KU-725-739

A CLASSICAL
EDUCATION

———

Richard Cobb

CHATTO & WINDUS
THE HOGARTH PRESS
LONDON

First published in 1985 by
Chatto & Windus · The Hogarth Press
40 William IV Street
London WC2N 4DF

All rights reserved. No part of this
publication may be reproduced, stored in a
retrieval system, or transmitted in any form,
or by any means, electronic, mechanical, photocopying,
recording or otherwise, without the prior
permission of the publisher.

British Library
Cataloguing in Publication Data
Cobb, Richard
A classical education.
I. Title
823'.914[F]   PR6053.O1/

ISBN 0 7011 2936 0

Copyright © Richard Cobb 1985

Photoset in Linotron Ehrhardt by
Rowland Phototypesetting Ltd
Bury St Edmunds, Suffolk
Printed in Great Britain by
Redwood Burn Ltd
Trowbridge, Wiltshire

Contents

To TIM HEALD

Preface

This book, or something vaguely like it, though very far from fully-grown, has been going around in my head for a good many years, perhaps from as far back as the early fifties. It hasn't been there all the time, pressing for recognition and immediate realisation, like an insistent and angry outbreak of literary toothache. There have been times when it disappeared altogether, from view and from mind, pushed back, if not under, by other more immediate preoccupations: my research in the French archives, the writing of articles in French provincial journals, the preparation of a long book on *Les Armées Révolutionnaires*, or the writing of subsequent studies on French history. Once I had gone into university teaching, at the age of thirty-eight, I came into touch with, first one generation, then another, of young people, first as a lecturer then as a tutor. Soon, I found myself readily identifying with the hopes, enthusiasms and preoccupations of people in their late teens and early twenties, to such an extent that I began living, as it were, at one stage removed, through their experiences and expectations, so that the memory of those that belonged to my *own* teens and early twenties were pushed well back in the queue, becoming much more remote. But the theme of the present book, though often disappearing altogether for long periods, would keep bobbing up, re-emerging as from an underground stream.

In nearly all my work as a historian, there has been a certain intermingling of history and autobiography. I have never succeeded in disentangling the two strands that have run through many of my books. But it has been only in the last three or four years, first writing

9

for Ronald Blythe's anthology *Places*, about my Cobb grandparents in Colchester, then evoking my childhood and adolescence in *Still Life: Sketches from a Tunbridge Wells Childhood*, that I have concentrated on a purely autobiographical approach, though, even then, I have tried to combine it with an awareness of time as well as of place and the co-existence of a more public history. I have found the experience agreeable and, once embarked on it, I have felt it very difficult to stop in mid-track. Why not go on along the same lines, while still *sur le lancer*? It was as if my present subject, in the direct wake of *Still Life*, and like the train from London as it approaches Tunbridge Wells Central, had all at once come out of the many murky tunnels through which it had been quietly travelling for as many as thirty years, to enjoy the full light of day.

This is a book primarily about two people: my old friend Edward, and myself, permanently fixed in a certain period of time during which our lives were often, but never always, closely related. We are not the only people in the book. There are many others. But the main subject is our relationship and our participation in a certain number of shared experiences and events, some of our own creation, others brought to bear on both of us by forces from outside, at least as I recall them. This is a very personal account, written from my own memories, such as they are, and often embellished by my own imagination. I have not aimed at absolute accuracy, being more concerned with readability; this is not a historical narrative, and I am not always sure at what stages fictional inventiveness takes over from the chronicle of memory. Additions have insisted on imposing their presence as I went along. I may have got some things wrong, left some things out, got other things in the wrong order. It is my version. There could be another one, or several others.

As on a previous occasion, I owe my grateful thanks to my wife, Margaret, and to my former pupil and friend, Roger Butler, both of whom, having had sections of the book read to them, have made suggestions as to how they could be improved, toned down, or shortened. Thanks to their critical comments, I have endeavoured to strip the narrative of all superfluities, giving, as I hope, the story a greater alertness and urgency. I would also like to thank the boys of one of the upper English forms of Rugby School for having laughed, with what appeared to be uncontrollable mirth, at one of the sections of the book that I tried out on them during a visit to the school.

My editor and friend, Hugo Brunner, who guided *Still Life* through all its stages, from blue Basildon Bond infancy in long hand, to final publication, has shown a similar patience, a similar forbearance and a similar sagacity on this occasion, taking the present book firmly by the arm in the final direction of the printer. I remember the old Everyman's series, each one opening with the words of Ernest Rhys about Everyman being a 'Guide, Philosopher & Friend'. Hugo is certainly the first and the third, as far as I am concerned. I would not know whether he is also the one in between, not being gifted with any understanding of abstract thought. This is my second book under his guidance. I hope there will be plenty more.

Wolvercote, 4 March, 1984

Gare Saint-Lazare

I was waiting at the barrier at the far right end of the Gare Saint-Lazare, near the post office and the exit leading down to the level of the rue du Havre. It was sometime in the spring of 1950. I have always liked that station, which seems to float in the air, high above the Quarter, once marshland, to which it has given its name; and there is no more exciting meeting place, especially if the meeting is for the first time, than in front of the huge war memorial at the far end of the immensely long *Salle des Pas Perdus*, the point of departure of many dreams and hopes. Facing the barrier and prominently displayed on the wall just behind me – I knew it by heart, it had greeted me so many times – was a large poster: 'When in Paris, Harry's New York Bar, SANK ROO DONOO' (an approximation of the address of that once-familiar establishment, 5, rue Daunou, near the Opéra). No doubt this was the first message of Paris that would catch the eye, as it was meant to, of wave after wave of American tourists just off the boat train from Le Havre or Cherbourg. I was meeting the former.

The train came in dead on time, the enormous engine showering steam from all its elaborately displayed guts, as if it had been turned inside-out, so that, for a moment, the passengers, as they approached the barrier, were partly hidden in the hot mist. I soon caught sight of Edward, towering above the others and striding out importantly, like a Foreign Minister walking towards the film cameras on his way to an international conference and with no time to stop. His head of reddish curly hair was as abundant as ever, his high-coloured face had broadened, while retaining its juvenile expression of surprise;

there was the same charming, welcoming smile in and around his very blue eyes, but he seemed to have put on a good deal of weight since I had last seen him nearly fourteen years before. He now looked quite hefty, and when he came level with me and started pumping my hand, greeting me in his beautifully modulated voice – he knew how to please and seldom failed to do so, especially on first encounter; but I think on this occasion his pleasure was quite genuine, as indeed was mine – I noticed that he had acquired the beginnings of a paunch. It is true that, for the last thirteen years, he had led a pretty sedentary existence; but he had never been very keen on physical exertion. He still looked very much like the schoolboy of years back, though blown up a bit.

I think, after our greetings, I got in first, telling him I wanted a full account, from start to finish: we had had to be careful about what we had put into letters, and there was so much to catch up on. His first words to me were surprising, though I should have known by then never to have been surprised by anything he said or did. 'What a pity,' he said, without a trace of that buoyant flippancy that had been very much part of his attraction, at least in my eyes, 'what a pity that we went to a classical school!' I was puzzled at this, for he had always referred to his father and to his mother under the names of a Greek god and a Greek goddess; so I asked him why it had been a pity. 'How would *you* wash an axe if it had traces of blood on it, and you wanted to remove the traces?' accompanying his question with one of his most engaging smiles, as if he were about to let me in on a delightful secret. 'I suppose I would boil some water and put the axe into it,' I replied. He looked at me triumphantly (he always liked being in the right) and said: 'Well, that is exactly what I did; and Chief Inspector Mahoney told me that that was just where I went wrong: it got the blood encrusted in the pores of the metal. He said I should have washed it in *cold* water, which would have left no trace.' He seemed quite genuinely aggrieved about this gap in our education, as if

Shrewsbury had let him down personally. This was typical of him, for he had always expected everything to be laid on, often at short notice or with no notice at all, for his own personal convenience. I said something like: 'Really, Edward, you could not have expected the school to have put on axe-washing classes just for your sole benefit; it was not a requirement of the syllabus, even if you had been on the Science Side, and you were on the Classical Side.' But this was to misunderstand Edward; *of course* Shrewsbury should have provided axe-washing classes, the school should have been able to look into the future and meet his later needs, when they arose. He was quite convinced of this. Why had he not been told at the time? What a lot of trouble would have been avoided if he had been properly taught! He was perfectly serious, and did not even realise that I was making fun of him.

He was incorrigible. I should not have been so surprised to find that he was as lacking in even a glimmer of self-awareness as ever. Why should he have changed, with all that time on his hands, with nothing to do but think about himself, about his own condition, about his changeless environment, about the unsuitability and uncouthness of some of his companions? ('Just peasants,' he was to complain later in the day, getting quite red in the face with indignation, 'brutes who had murdered their wives with scythes and that sort of thing, anything that came to hand.') He had been so preoccupied with his own situation that outside events had largely passed him by: the Popular Front, Munich, the war and its aftermath, the beginnings of the cold war. There was even something reassuring about his changelessness, his simple, unquestioning self-centredness: still the same old Edward, in a slightly enlarged version, that was all. His steadfast egotism seemed to offer a sort of refuge in a sea of uncertainty. For the moment, we were both back at the beginning: two schoolboys at Rigg's in our two-boy act of provocation, the enjoyment of a coded language designed to exclude others and the

15

preparation and the realisation of noisy assaults on the solemnities of collective conformisms.

It was very nice to be together again, after all these years, though, of course, they had not weighed as heavily on myself as on my friend. There was nothing much likely to endanger my enjoyment of the moment. I could, after all, ration my encounters with Edward; one needed to space them out, otherwise he could become an awful bore. I had plenty of other friends and activities that would have been quite unfamiliar to him. His clock had stopped in 1936, whereas a great many things had happened to me since then. But, for the moment, I was quite happy to find myself renewing my compère act. Edward had, after all, been largely my discovery, and this seemed as good an occasion as any to get him to display his somewhat limited talents. The opportunity for this, I thought, would come that evening over the dinner table, when we would be assured of an audience, some of which would understand English; and both Edward and I had loud, confident public school voices. There had always been a strong element of showmanship and provocation in our relations, I taking the part of a sort of *montreur*, and Edward responding with eager enthusiasm, as we both became more and more excited by the realisation that an increasing number of people were listening to our exchanges which were not designed to be private.

This is in fact exactly what had happened in the restaurant – a large and rather gaudy affair with seats in red plush along the walls, off the rue Marbeuf – that same evening – as Edward, guided by my frequent promptings and requests that he go back over that particular bit of ground again, gave his blow-by-blow account in happy, ringing tones that created around us spreading eddies and rippling circles of horrified silence, as even knives and forks were stilled. Some people called for their bills and started to leave hurriedly, as Edward's voice gained volume, interrupted every now and then by fits of uncontrollable giggles, his face quite purple and his blue eyes watering with merriment. This was inevitably a star performance, as it was the first time we had been back in the act together for a very long time. But there would be many others; and, with each repeat, our standards improved, or so it seemed to me. Edward was, after all, something of a rarity, and I quite enjoyed displaying him. On each of these occasions the years rolled back, and, almost unconsciously, we resumed, well on into our thirties and forties, our dual bit of schoolboy fooling. Some people never grow up; Edward was one, and, in his company, especially in public places, I soon found myself shaking with gust after gust of irresistible adolescent laughter, choking over the wine, the tears falling into my plate. Edward's quite childlike merriment had always been extremely infectious. I have had other partners in this sort of game later in life but between Edward and myself there remained a mutual triggering-off process that would start off quite calmly and soberly, gather speed, and culminate in quite helpless fits of hilarity, as we shook like jellies over our plates. Edward was a perfect partner in these somewhat indecent games, because I could always be quite certain of his responses; he had the reliability of a perfectly tuned instrument. Shocking perhaps, certainly in the worst possible taste; but we just could not help it, a single glance between us would be enough to set us off.

I remember listening once to two old Saumurois in their eighties, as each evoked, in the semi-coded language and vigorous military slang of nineteen-year-old cavalry cadets, some of the pranks that the two of them had got up to while training at their illustrious school. The transformation was immediate and startling; out of the window went the ponderousness of two staid retired generals, while the room rang with peals of juvenile laughter, as, pushing and jostling one another – *tiens, tu te souviens* . . . ? – they reduced themselves to heaving gusts of uncontrollable merriment, while I listened on in amazement at the suddenness and totality of the transformation. There they were, actually back at Saumur together, over a gap of sixty years, with everything in between erased: promotion, marriage, children, successes and failures. It was the same with Edward and myself, every time we met in public and in the awareness of an audience that needed to be stimulated and provoked. It did not matter where it was: Paris, Brussels, Oxford. Before many minutes were up, there we were, quite speechless with mirth, two silly boys in a grim and humourless house, back at Shrewsbury, participating in what was in fact perfectly innocent fun, for we were innocent in the fullness of our common enjoyment; there was no malice in it: just schoolboy fun, nothing more. I suppose that if I were blameworthy, it was because I tended to use Edward as an instrument of my own amusement. But he was always very willing to be used, indeed, enjoyed being used; and he had so few friends that he clung, rather pathetically, to the memory of our two-boy act; and each such repeat performance represented for him a temporary escape from loneliness. And he *was* very lonely, very wary of strangers. He had so few subjects of conversation, and though he possessed a natural politeness and a great ability to please, to the point of charm, he had little to say, and, when in company, was soon liable to lapse into sulky silence. I believe that it was only with me, and under my prodding, that he could feel himself a complete person. I make him sound like some sort of performing clown, which he was not. Somewhere behind the façade of giggles there existed a person who was rather unhappy; I have often wondered how he got through the day alone with his confused thoughts. For the last few years, I had, till very recently, avoided seeing him, or even replying to his letters, despite many timid overtures on his part.

But, dwelling on the excitement generated in both of us by the sudden resumption of our relationship, following so long a break, I have quite failed to mention a side of Edward that was revealed to me for the first time on that memorable day: an Edward far removed from my familiar partner in schoolboy clowning, an adult now who, after all, had matured in suffering and who had acquired, as a result of deprivation, a quality of wonder and sheer joy of which I would have thought him quite incapable. Now it seemed that he was not as incomplete as I had believed, that perhaps he had even moved beyond 1936. We talked – or rather he talked, and I listened, right through the afternoon, in a quiet, rather dark café where, as I remember, people were playing chess and card games. He referred most movingly to the sheer wonderment of his first fortnight of liberty, of the gradually unfolding awareness that he was free to go where he wanted and as far as he liked, that there were no locked doors or high walls with barbed wire along the top; and to the marvellous realisation that he could walk to the next crossroads, then to the one after that, that he could follow on foot an avenue of trees to its very end, coming out in the open beyond, that he could enjoy a multiplicity of landscapes, urban and rural, provided for his exclusive enjoyment, that all this visual wealth lay ahead of him, and that all he had to do was to walk through it and enjoy it. He told me that it had been the most momentous fortnight in his whole life, that he found he could not tire of the ever-changing scene, could hardly believe the diversity of images that were being offered him, that, for the first time in thirteen years, the word *vista* acquired a concrete meaning, and that he could walk towards a constantly changing series of perspectives, as if, like Alice, he had been moving across a monster chess-board. What struck him as the most marvellous gift was this ability all at once to see *beyond*.

For all those years he had been enclosed, hemmed in, by an immobile landscape, with every detail of which he had become wearisomely familiar: not *quite* immobile, perhaps, for the clouds would move, the trees would bend to the gale, the sky would darken with snow or with the rain, the colours would change with the seasons, and he could see further in winter than in the spring or summer, but even so a restricted landscape. There had been no *beyond*, no means even of imagining what did in fact lie beyond, just a painted landscape on a backdrop: a hill that concealed for ever its far side, a valley that petered out in dark shadow, a road that exhausted itself on its first bend, half a house with only windows, the other half, with the front-door, invisible, trees that had tops that waved gently in the breeze, but no trunks, no visible means of support, a pattern of farm roofs that appeared to be floating, with their walls cut off, a copse of evergreens that screened from view a wider horizon. Of course, if he stood on a chair, he could enlarge the picture a little at the bottom; if he put the chair to the right, he could get in a little more on that side, then a little bit on the left could similarly be added on; and as his room had three windows, the first to the west, the other two to the north, he had the choice of two quite different pictures. Jacques-Louis David might have made something of the double aspect, as he had for a single one: his painting of the Luxembourg Gardens in the autumn, the trees turning, under a grey sky, as seen from his long prison dormitory at the very top of the Palace; but the French painter had looked out on this scene, as viewed from a height – an interesting exercise in perspective – for only a few months, before once more commanding the broad sweep of the Seine, the regimented trees of the raised terrace of the Tuileries, and the crowded houses lining the quays on the Right Bank, the barges and the laundry boats, the river baths, the landing stages, from his airy studio high up in the Louvre; and, if he got sick of that, he could go down and wander in the Paris streets. But Edward's view had been much more limited. He had had to make do with his two truncated pictures, only narrowly extendable at the edges and the bottom, from the level of a movable chair, for thirteen years (and, for all he knew at the time, for much longer).

And then, all at once, he had discovered that, if he wished, he could simply walk through the two old canvases, tearing them asunder, walk through the torn splits, and push ahead, as far as his feet – or a bicycle, a horse, a car, a train – would take him. As I listened to his wonderfully eloquent account of a whole world opening up before his astonished eyes, the expression *prendre la clef des champs* seemed to take on a new, quite tangible meaning. He had not found the key hanging up behind a secret door; it had been given to him, and it had opened up, not just fields, but the whole unrolling landscape. He told me that, in the first two or three weeks he had spent back in England, he had done little else other than walk and look, catching up on the visual deprivation, the monotony of two narrow canvases, of all those years of immobility, stunned, delighted, overwhelmed by the sheer variety of everything, by size, space, perspective and distance, by the limitless range of choice so gener-ously offered him by the possession of the magic key, according to which direction he took: houses, streets, parks, woods, hills, lakes, rivers, valleys, churches, church spires, markets, stations, quays, railway lines, feasting his starved eyes on such profusion, and always pushing forward in the anticipated delight of commanding yet another horizon. He told me that anything indicating distance caused him particular excitement: railway lines as seen from a bridge, a great river as it broadened out towards the sea, even an ugly main road as viewed from a hill as it disappeared in a dusty distance, an avenue of poplars. He often got lost, he *liked* getting lost, not knowing where he was, and trying to work his way backwards. Getting lost was a luxury almost forgotten, hidden away somewhere in the distant memory of adolescent mobility. Now it could be deliberately rediscovered and savoured as the priceless gift of mobil-ity and freedom. He walked, he sat on the top of buses, not knowing where they would take him, buying a ticket to the terminus; he got on river boats, he took suburban trains, he went to the sea. He spent most of his waking hours on the move, rediscovering the forgotten wonders of the night: the inky silence of a small wood, the stealthy rustling sounds of a copse, the lines of street lamps, the patterns of lighted windows throwing moving figures in black silhouette, the blaze thrown on a wide pavement by the brightly lit windows of a huge public house, the winking coloured signals of a terminus, the silver gleam of converging railway lines, the coloured moving letters of huge advertisements flicking across tall buildings and throwing faintly coloured reflections on the ground, lighting up, green, red, mauve, the faces of pedestrians, the red lights outlining a wireless mast or a pylon, the dark dome of a cathedral picked out in moonlight, the brilliant glare of a market, the flickering lights of a distant shore the far side of a dark black river, the moving squares of yellow light of a train as it crossed a bridge, the tall lighted windows, row upon row, of a great hospital, the flurry of lights from a newspaper office, the indistinct glow – merely a slight lightening of the surrounding cotton wool – of lights seen through fog. I think that, in the state of euphoria in which he then found himself, he would even have welcomed the searching fingers of wartime caressing the night sky, the fireworks of anti-aircraft fire, though I cannot say, for this was something – and there are degrees in misfortune – that had remained outside his visual experience. If he had had the strength I think he would have walked through the night, as he had walked through the day, with pauses only for meals, so urgently did he feel the need to catch up on time lost, as if, if he were not quick to pounce on it, all this wealth might suddenly be snatched from his gaze.

He told me that he had worn through a new pair of shoes in that wonderful and tireless first fortnight (and there was to be little slowing up later, for, during the fortnight that followed and that he spent with me in Paris, I had difficulty in keeping up with his implacable pace as we crossed the city from Clignancourt to the Porte d'Orléans, from Boulogne to Vincennes; we were both in need of new soles and heels), a fortnight spent rediscovering what seemed to him a world reborn, refurbished and freshly painted in bright, inviting colours, as if, at thirty-three, he had been re-endowed with the round eyes of a wondering child, with the amazement, endless curiosity and visual retentiveness of a four-year-old, for whom all the flowers appear to be in perpetual bloom. He said that he had never previously experienced such unmitigated joy, such an exhilarating sense of renewal, at least as far as his eyes were concerned. He had at first been rather frightened by the sheer volume of noise, by the bustle and the pushing of the busy crowds; he had marvelled at the landscape, but had felt threatened by the people who moved in it: there were too many of them. He had not been used to crowds, had hardly ever been confronted with strange faces, and had felt very conspicuous, as if any passer-by could have recognised in this energetic red-haired figure someone who had come from outside and who did not quite belong to the rush and urgency of the working day in a big city. And they would have been quite right: he was so visibly an onlooker, one who paused and stopped, hesitated in his progress and turned round, as if uncertain of what direction to take. What business did he have wandering about sight-seeing in the middle of February, was the question he seemed to read in their surprised or disapproving glances.

So unaccustomed had he become to communicating in public, that he had felt timid in restaurants, afraid not to be able to cope with the proffered menu; he had not been too sure of the right order of words; he had heard himself talking too softly or raising his voice to a pitch of impatience and truculence when ordering a drink in a public-house; he had become aware, by the amusement he provoked in barmen, that he was speaking in a slang that was years out of date. For the first few days he had had an uneasy feeling that people had been looking at him in a special sort of knowing way, as if they had been able to read the secret of the previous thirteen years, and had spotted, in the manner of his walking, in his indeterminate gait and in the way he kept glancing behind him, as if to reassure himself that he was not being followed, a person who had lost the self-confidence of someone who could at once account for his presence in that particular place at that particular time and who was clearly about his legitimate business. He told me that, in the presence of crowds, he had the impression of re-living the slow-moving, patient and unrelenting nightmare of his last days of freedom, in another, much more compact city, nearly fourteen years previously. Then he had been able to walk freely throughout the place, go out to the suburbs and look up friends, sit in the parks, step out along the cliffs; but, wherever he went, and whenever he looked behind him, there were always the same three figures, in hats and shabby belted mackintoshes, keeping their even distance behind him, stopping when he stopped, getting up when he got up, or progressing at his own steady pace, and making no effort to keep out of sight, as if indeed they intended him to spot them. If he left his home at any time in the morning, they would be standing at a street corner thirty yards from his door; if he went into a bank or a shop, they would be waiting, not just outside, but a few doors down. If he went into a public-house for a drink, he could see them, through the elaborate wall-mirrors with gilded writing on them, sitting in another bar, with their drinks in front of them. He had tried the darkness of a cinema in the belief that the obscurity might shake them off, but, as he came out, at the end of the performance, or even a little before the end, he could see the three getting up and putting on their hats, a few rows behind. He had supposed that they had kept up the vigil throughout the night, had indeed taken a look through the top of the glazed window of the bathroom at three in the morning, and had made out three figures standing right under a nearby street light. But, after the first fortnight, these fears had left him, and he had grown at last secure in the knowledge of his unbreached anonymity. He was *not* being followed, no one was in the least bit interested in him, there was no awakening curiosity in the eyes of the casual passer-by. He had still felt some embarrassment when someone engaged him in conversation in a bar or in some public place, for he was afraid of displaying his ignorance of public events and of a national experience believed to be shared. Momentous happenings had reached him in a muted or garbled form over the previous thirteen years. He had not known about rationing, had been safe from military service, had not experienced air raids, had no views about Hitler or Stalin, little more than names to him. On such occasions, he had tried to deflect the course of the conversation by saying that he had been living abroad and had only just returned. And, strictly speaking, this had been true.

By the time I saw him, and he'd told me about the joy of pushing further and further *beyond*, he had shed all these fears and had fully recovered his self-confidence and his normal rather amiable bounce. Being in Paris was a great help. How could the French have been able to pick him out from any other Anglo-Saxon tourist, with his atrocious accent, his tweed sports coat, his grey flannels and his stout walking-shoes? His stay in the city completed the process of recuperation and adjustment to freedom, while his eagerness to explore, to push into *passages* and courtyards, to climb steep steps, to take in everything, was as strong and as inexhaustible as it had been in that first delirious fortnight. I don't think I have ever met a more enthusiastic tourist, nor a more grateful one. He was constantly thanking me, as if I had laid on the whole of Paris exclusively for his benefit (he probably thought that I had, for he was in the habit always of personalising everything that came anywhere near him). He was most agreeable company, as he still could not contain his joy in his recovered mobility, bubbling over with excitement and enthusiasm. In the course of these walks, which took up most of the daylight hours during his visit, I discovered an aspect of Edward the existence of which I had been previously quite unaware: an adult both very observant and of unfailing aesthetic judgment, one who knew where to look and how to look, quick to comment on the lightness of the sky of the Ile-de-France, the broadness of the perspectives, the openness of the countryside, or to remark on the Utrillo-like quality and texture of the grey leprous walls of steep houses. He delighted in the sights and sounds of the Paris markets and proved unexpectedly sensitive to the stresses and the intonations of spoken French. He was fascinated by the newness and the unfamiliarity of everything and insisting on travelling the full length of every single *métro* line, commenting on the bizarre or poetical names of some of the stations (*Filles de Calvaire* was a special favourite, but he liked the hell-fire undertones of *Sèvres-Babylone*, and enjoyed the tongue-twisting sound of *Barbès-Rochechouart*). He derived as much boyish enjoyment from seeing the streets and avenues unrolling themselves in reverse from the open back platform of a bus. I had never previously found him such good company. He seemed to have acquired a second sight and to have learnt to distinguish what was visually significant. Of course, each evening, as if the going had been too hard, the other Edward, my schoolboy partner, would take over, and soon we would be both back in the double act, convulsed with giggling, our voices getting louder and louder.

It was not so much that he had changed, rather that he had doubled himself, so that now there were two Edwards existing, side by side, apparently without communicating. The wonderful gift of mobility had not merely given him a new lease of life, dispersing his natural lethargy, it had enriched him with an alternative personality, more mature, more retentive, less self-centred. This new, energetic Edward was, from this Paris trip onwards – and there would be plenty more of those – firmly set on a steadily more ambitious programme of travel that would take him, in the course of the next thirty years or so, further and further south and east (he showed no interest in the north, and the west, well . . . that was out). I think he may have regarded me as in some way the creator of this new version of himself – the avid tourist, the insistent traveller, the tireless visitor to galleries and museums, the red-faced angry man insisting on having closed places opened up after hours for his inspection, guidebook and wallet in hand – because I had walked him around Paris and had listened, with undisguised fascination, to his tale of wonder, during the afternoon of that first day in the city, when he had enthralled and deeply moved me with his description of the joy of recovered mobility.

Certainly, as far as I could make out, *beyond* was still the goal; but it was getting further and further away. I had set him going, first in Paris, then in Brussels; but, after that, growing every year in confidence, he was taking off more and more on his own. I don't think at this time he ever travelled with a companion, that was to come much later. It would have been a mistake to have done so, at least at this early, exploratory stage; it would have ended in unholy rows, for he liked to get his own way, and either sulked or flew into a rage when he didn't. I think at the time he had sufficient self-knowledge to realise that it was wiser for him to travel on his own. In any case, it would have been hard to have found anyone who would have been prepared to share what appeared to be an increasingly punishing programme. It was only much later in life, when the pace had slackened and he had grown more urbane, more tolerant and easy-going that he started to travel with a companion. I was even quite surprised to have heard of this apparently uncharacteristic experiment. But, from what he told me, it seemed to be working most harmoniously. In my rather summary judgment on him I had not sufficiently allowed for change, for a more relaxed approach to travel.

Sharing, then, no. But a sort of sharing kept at a safe, generally considerable, distance. He had always been very anxious to impress me, and now he was very keen to keep me *au fait* with his progress as a seasoned traveller. Like another Mr Norris (*he* also had a past to escape from and a need to distance himself from a certain number of places), over the years he would bombard me with picture postcards

– the picture was not the thing, but the exotic stamp and the postmark in queer letters – from places like Sofia, Cairo, Bucharest, Prague, Bayreuth (year after year, in communion with Wagner), Moscow, Kiev, Leningrad, Odessa, Palermo, Warsaw, Prague, Naples, Madrid, Lisbon, Oporto, Barcelona, Algiers. The cards would carry only the tersest of messages, in his schoolboy scrawl (an area where the two Edwards were temporarily reunited): 'Wonderful weather here', 'Cold but crisp', 'Fantastic wooden churches', 'Went to High Mass', 'Just off to Vesuvius', 'The Acropolis disappointing', 'Food as bad as at Rigg's', 'A marvellous mosque', 'A boring, shabby place', 'Couldn't sleep a wink for the heat', 'An appalling hotel', 'The staff surly and rude', 'Coming back here next year', 'I don't recommend this'. The messages were just pretexts. He wanted me to know that he was once more on the move, that he had taken in yet another place, that he had *been to* this or that. He still needed an audience, if only of one, and one at the receiving end of a crudely coloured postcard, the sky a bright pink, the foliage a spinach green, the buildings a sickly yellow, the clouds like puffs of cotton wool. Discomfort seemed to be the main theme of the brief signals that he sent out as he moved from place to place, so that I could chart his peregrinations and try and make out what mysterious grand scheme could lie behind their apparently often haphazard course. I think he had a reasonable private income, so he could well afford these jaunts. He was certainly making up for all the years of immobility. I wonder where the next card will come from: Debrecen? Ankara? Ljubljana? Timisoara? Łuck? It would have to be something like that, for he has exhausted all the capitals, most of the active volcanoes, pretty well all the opera-houses, most of the casinos. Wherever it is from, I'll promise to be impressed.

2

The House Photograph

The small boys are in the front row, sitting cross-legged on the ground with their hands cupping their knees, their Eton collars covering the tops of their dark blue suits. I am towards the right end of the row. I look rather sly, like a fox wearing a bib. I am not looking directly at the camera, but with my eyes slightly down, as if hovering nervously between the ground and the photographer. In contrast to the other small cross-legged boys whose eyes look straight ahead, as if witnessing both to their innocence and to their self-confidence, as if they had no need to apologise for being in that group, I appear shifty and a bit out of place. Pitt, even smaller than myself, stares out boldly; Wilson has a vague smirk, barely contained; Gillespie, too, seems quite sure of himself; Chant, who is very good-looking, is smiling; Bower looks out innocently from beneath his abundant curls. One of the boys in this group, wearing horn-rims, has the smooth face of a choirboy, very chubby, even fat. He looks as if he has to put up with quite a lot and that he can take it in good heart, or at least put a good face on it.

The next row, seated on chairs, consists of the power élite: Mr Haydon, the white-haired housemaster, the head of house, who looks – and is – gentle and nice, and the monitors. One of the monitors, a self-satisfied expression on his brutal prize-fighter's face, lounges, rather than sits, as if to emphasise that he regards the whole procedure as a rather ridiculous time-loser when he might be so much better employed beating the Eton collar brigade in the front row. His neighbour – and visible companion in crime, supplying the refinement and imaginative cruelty to supplement the other's sheer brute strength – has greasy black crinkly hair and pouches under his eyes, which are (as I know) a muddy brown. He looks corrupt and dissipated, as well as cruel. The pair stand out among the other fairly innocuous, even decent, faces of the privileged row, a row that bodes ill for the near future, for both the benevolent-looking elderly housemaster and the pleasant-faced head of house are in their last year, and the hideous succession is visible to one side of them. The liberal era will soon be at an end, the reign of the bullies is almost visibly imminent. The row of crossed-legs is in for a bad time; the row of crossed-legs that will be in the front of next year's photograph will be in for an even worse one. Bully-Face and Crinkly Corruption have only to bide their time, as they smirk at the camera. The future would look bleaker still had the photograph contained the ferret-like face of the housemaster-to-be, the son-in-law of the old man in the dark suit. Ferret-Face will be no match for the bully-boy pair. Indeed, he will encourage them.

The row behind, standing, consists of fairly tall, fully-developed boys, fifteen, sixteen and seventeen, mostly in hard collars with pointed corners. They appear quite affable, with a not-caring-too-much look, a vague *insouciance*, as if they have floated above the trivialities of collective formalities. They have every reason to look as they do, for they are virtually unpunishable, and know it. The faces in this row are still blank, unmarked by power and brutality or by benevolence and kindness. The faces are still waiting to be filled in; this will happen within a year or two. Meanwhile, there is a pleasant, almost frivolous, uncertainty about them. One of them is grinning broadly, as if the whole thing is quite hilarious. He has brushed-down hair (red, in fact, though this is not shown). Not that he stands out particularly, save for his height and the broadness of his grin; indeed, he may even be laughing, and some of his neighbours have strained looks around the corners of their mouths, as if they are having a hard time containing themselves. Perhaps the tall fellow, who looks a charmer, has just whispered a joke to those nearest to him.

The back row is standing on a bench. They are rather hard to place, a mixed bag with no common element, a jumble of collars rounded at the edges, and pointed ones. There seems to be the same discrepancy about their ages and their height as about their collars; some resemble the cross-legged children, but standing up, as if they had just learnt this position; others appear to be stuck awkwardly halfway between childhood and adolescence, holding themselves gawkily, not quite knowing what to do with their hands and with their heads at an angle or looking to the side, as if to take a cue from a neighbour. The photograph does not actually reveal such details, but it is likely that some of them have spotty faces.

What is striking about all these faces is the absence of fear, the confidence, even the serenity (the bullies excepted). It is true that I look decidedly uneasy, keeping my head well down and doing my best not to eye the camera full face; but this is due to shyness, rather than to plain funk. All seem to look confidently towards the future, as to something that is their *due*, something to be taken for granted. The bullies have every reason to; their immediate future is already quite plainly marked in the creases of cruelty and low cunning that line their faces, as if they have aged prematurely. Gillespie looks calm and resolute, his eyes are clear and unflinching, there is no visible warning of the breakdown to come a year later, at the height of the new regime. Clover is scratching his leg, he is ungainly and has about him an air of sagacity, as if he is already an adult, and could be the child of elderly parents – his father, as I was to discover, was a retired clergyman who lived in Cambridge. But his curiously old face also reflects unruffled confidence. Collingwood also has rather a learned look, accentuated by steel spectacles; but, again, there is nothing to suggest the imminence of breakdown. Little Pitt has a very knowing face, and one who will listen, watch, step with care. Chant and

Wilson look honest and perfectly open; Chant is good-natured, and will take a lot of ragging with a patient, tolerant smile; he is allowed a cushion during evening prep, because he gets boils on his bottom. Pullan has a comic face and is also afflicted with the Christian name of Hiram, which he jokes about; in the photograph, he displays a lopsided grin that seems to apologise for itself, for him and for his Christian name. His good-naturedness is quite visible. The elder Neild looks a bit worried, as if he had forgotten something; his younger brother looks benevolent and calm. He is certainly not a worrier. Redfern, sitting on the ground, is ferret-faced, like the housemaster-elect (they are both Unitarians, and will get on well together, as members of the ferret family). The faces all do give away quite a lot: gawkiness, timidity, shyness, shrewdness, calculation, *insouciance*, intelligence, reflection, brutality, vulgarity, kindness, generosity, innocence, decency, depravity. But none displays fear.

Of course, like bad history, it is easy to be wise after the event. The photograph was taken in 1932. Within ten years or a little more, the owners of half-a-dozen of the faces would be dead. As it happened, the bullies and the thugs all survived but poor, awkward Clover, with his large beak of a nose and his old man's face, was shot by the Italians; the good-natured Chant, and Pullan, with his impossible Christian name and his lopsided grin – they only put his initials on the house war memorial – were killed. No doubt most of those who survived had careers that were fairly predictable, succeeding their fathers in the family business, in a profession, or in the Army. The younger Neild became a doctor, because he was a dutiful son, his father was a doctor, and his elder brother did not want to do medicine; one of them had to. Collingwood, the son of a Professor, seemed bound for academic life; but Gillespie, badly wounded by the Japanese, gave little hint of eventually becoming a Professor of German. The bullies presumably went on being bullies; it would be hard to think that, having set out so badly, their faces already marked by a quite adult cruelty, they could have undergone a change of heart. But group photographs give away so little. Think of those of Tsarist Russia in the years before 1914: a banquet, the men in white ties, the women in enormous feathered hats, their deep black eyes appearing intense in the cameras; a school group, very stiff in their uniforms, their peaked caps held on their knees, the frock-coated teacher sitting in the middle, bearded and with a pince-nez; a stately game of tennis, in a clearing, with a background of silver birch, female servants in black and white uniforms bringing in little trays and samovars for tea; a regimental photograph, a great deal of gold and silver braid in squiggly patterns down the front of uniforms, eyes somewhat stoned, and international military faces with an international assortment of moustaches, waxed or drooping. We cannot read in any of these prints the fate of those thus displayed, we cannot read in their expressions – vacuous, joyful, festive, drunken, pompous, youthful, mournful, pensive, good-looking, self-satisfied, well-fed, vicious, satiated, awkward, intelligent, sensitive – even a trace of foreboding, a hint of the horrors to come. Just as well, too. It is the same with the photograph of the boys of Rigg's Hall, No. 1 the Schools. There is no premonition of violent death on the faces of Chant, Clover and Pullan. Nor could the tall boy in the back row, looking uncharacteristically solemn, have foreseen his own uncommon fate. Or perhaps he did already have a hint of it, for he always liked to think of himself as 'different', as quite out of the ordinary; and from the very first time I met him, I remarked on his tendency to dramatise even the most banal incident and, above all, to blow up to vastly inflated proportions any event that concerned him personally. Perhaps the strangest thing about him is that his eager smile, his capacity for laughter, his ready, slightly excessive enthusiasms, and his elaborate, slightly overdone manner of greeting, are almost identical, at sixty-eight, to that of the good-looking, open-faced boy of sixteen, standing on the back row of the photograph.

33

3

The Study

On my first day at Rigg's Hall, I was put in the study of the head of house, a pleasant, civilised, gentle-voiced Lowland Scot called Bruce Urquhart, with the result that I was fairly safe from the immediate attention of the two bullies. It was a long, narrow room, more like a corridor, with one window very high up at the end, so that there was little natural light and those who were further in had to rely on artificial light all through the day. Perhaps it had originally been a corridor, or had been formed by having an intermediary wall put in to divide it from the main corridor, lined halfway up with chocolate-coloured lavatory brick, topped with a seedy beige wash, just outside, where all the house notices were put up: 'Everyone will voluntarily attend the match against Moser's this afternoon at 2.30', and similar exhortations compulsorily to do things out of one's own free will.

There were five or six desks set at right angles to the window, that of the head of house being the furthest inside and consequently the darkest. Mine was about halfway down. I cannot remember who had the desk to my left, but on my right there was a tall boy with red curly hair, very blue eyes, and a most winning smile. He noticed, on that very first day, that I was reading *A Pair of Blue Eyes*: 'Do you mind if I say something?', he said, in a voice that seemed to reflect genuine concern. 'It is all right *here*, but you need to be careful in this hell-hole' (meaning, I suppose, Rigg's), 'I'll lend you some yellow Crime Club covers, then they won't spot what you are actually reading.' He went on to say that he was in his second year and knew the ropes, adding that his name was Edward, and inquiring what mine was, for he didn't want to call me Cobb. I was heartened by this

34

show of interest and said that I was called Richard. My friend – for so he proved at once to be – offered his services and his protection; he would help me with the Colour Exams and I could count on his advice on how to get round the many calls to collective conformism and the display of tribal loyalties. From what he said, he seemed already quite proficient in defeating what he referred to as 'the system', an occupation that seemed to take up a great deal of his time, for he went on to tell me that he had no interest in sport and found class-room work rather boring, though it did have the advantage of getting one out of Hell-Hole. I was touched by his direct approach, which seemed quite disinterested, for I was not at all good-looking, and I was grateful for his readily proffered protection: he did seem a powerful and useful ally.

He went on to tell me that Urquhart was a good chap, but that one of the boys in the study, two up from me, spied for the bullies and that I should be particularly careful about what I said to him, adding that I should always keep my desk shut when I went out. He went through the whole membership of the house, from monitors down to two-year-olds (of which he was one), dividing the boys up into utter philistines, philistines, crypto-philistines, time-servers and runners with the pack, informers, and open or clandestine wreckers of the system. He seemed to regard himself as an open wrecker. Later, when I knew him better, I came to the conclusion that temperamentally he was unsuited to the sort of clandestine activity that soon became one of my favourite means of survival. He went at things like a bull and was quite incapable of concealing his feelings, whereas I had always been quite good at appearing to agree with those whom I deeply disliked and at affecting a genuine show of enthusiasm for activities that I found intensely boring. Unlike Clover or Gillespie, who often attacked the system head on, I was a born survivor, knowing when to keep my head well down and how to conceal my likes and dislikes. My relationship with my friendly neighbour to the right soon developed on the basis of an unconscious pooling of resources. He was always prepared to undertake anything, however outrageous – indeed, the more outrageous the better – whereas I counselled caution, dissimulation, and the advantages of an oblique approach. By the end of the first week, we had worked out the basis of a profitable partnership.

There was more to it than a common dislike of the accepted orthodoxies and the elaboration of means of subverting them, though, of course, in this sort of closed, inbred society, they were a powerful link. But it was not enough of a link for our partnership to develop much further from there. I found in the school, as well as in the town (when I could get there) the best escape from the house; and most of my interests were in the classroom. This was not the case with Edward, who had few outside activities, and who, as a result, could become quite obsessed with Hell-Hole, giving it an import-ance the rather seedy place did not merit. I was far too cautious to become deeply involved in his very overt acts of defiance. But I found Edward wonderfully amusing, his total irreverence was brac-ing, and I was at once tickled by his habit of always referring to his father and his mother as 'Moloch' and 'Medea'. It was only two or three years later that I discovered that his father, a very eminent consultant, was called Charles; what his mother's Christian name was I have only discovered very recently and not from him. But, once I had met her for the first time, I thought that Medea suited her admirably, defining her in one word.

I liked his constant tendency to exaggeration; there was a sort of schoolboy gusto about the way he laid it on. He certainly made his bizarre family sound wonderfully exciting: there always seemed to be some drama going on, mostly involving the incessant hostilities, conducted from one end of Dublin to the other, and even out into the suburbs, waged, with apparent equal enthusiasm, by his parents, who had lived apart ever since 1927. The warfare seemed so all-consuming that I wondered how his father had time to look after his extensive practice. Every time a letter came from Dublin, Edward would have more to add to the chronicle of family rows. It would seem that they all – not just his father and his mother – lived in a perpetual atmosphere of bad melodrama. There was an aunt, who called herself Madame Roussel, and who wrote excessively bad novels under that name; I still possess one of them, a lurid tale of sin and redemption that had at the time met with the enthusiastic approval of the Roman Catholic Archbishop of Dublin. Madame Roussel had also aspired to the stage, but, like the rest of the family (and Edward himself), she over-acted appallingly and had failed even more completely in her would-be theatrical career than as a novelist.

His father, it appeared, had a mistress, whom he also employed as a nurse; but his house was run by his sister, in so far as she was capable of running anything, because she was seldom sober. Back home there seems never to have been a dull moment; there was always a crisis developing or erupting. The public chronicles of his family's rows gave Edward a sort of prestige throughout the house. It was his one wealth. Of course he exploited them for all he was worth, it was the one thing that distinguished him from the rest of us, most of whom, as far as I could judge, had parents who were quite uninterestingly normal. Nor was it all exaggeration. At the end of each term, the housemaster would get two telegrams, one from each parent, insisting that Edward be sent to his or her home; all the housemaster could do was to see that the boy got on the boat at Holyhead; what happened the other end was beyond his powers. But Edward would bask in this thrice-yearly added drama, commenting, as he often did: 'There will be a drama in my family, one day.' It seemed to me, at the time, that there was one already, and that it had been a very long-running show. I suppose Edward felt the need to give it an extra nudge.

After a term next to Edward, I felt that I already knew Moloch and Medea, familiar twin demons, as well as a cluster of aunts in supporting roles; and I looked forward to the opportunity of actually meeting one of them, or both, though not of course together. It appeared that the one or the other would be coming over for the next speech day in the following June; but each was keeping his or her plans secret, so that he would not know which parent would turn up on the actual day. As it turned out, however, each having delayed to the last possible moment in an endeavour to penetrate the secret of the other's plans, that summer, rather than risking meeting on the boat, or worse, in one of the marquees set up for speech day, they were to cancel each other out. Neither of them turned up. Edward had few descriptive powers, so that his parents remained in my imagination disembodied, emblematic figures, forces of evil no doubt, of superhuman malevolence, but denied recognisable physical features. Beyond asserting that Medea was rather more awful than Moloch, he could offer few details by which to distinguish them. He did say that his mother had been rather good-looking, before she had taken to the bottle in a big way, adding that she would certainly lay on the charm when seeking to trap someone. Yes, I would see, she would probably charm me. I think he was actually keen to display her to me (and to his other closer friends in the house), if only to show that he had not been exaggerating. He had quite a proprietary attitude towards her, as if she had been his own creation. It would have been a sort of triumph for him if she revealed herself as truly as awful as he had made out. Edward seemed quite confident that she would; but I was afraid that she might not come up to expectations. He was even hazier about his father, save that he had a foul temper and eyes that nearly popped out of his head, and that he was considerably older than his estranged wife. As I never met him, I have never been able to put a face on him. But Edward, who was a bit of a snob, was quite fond of talking about his father's family, pointing out that his grandfather, who had been knighted, had been at one time Director of Dublin Zoo; and he let it be known that, on the paternal side, he came of an Ascendancy family. Indeed, it was from him that I first heard the word 'Ascendancy' used.

Of course, one could have too much of the two Ms. There were days when I was quite fed up hearing about them; it seemed a schoolboy game that could easily become tedious. The trouble was Edward had little else to offer and I had much more in common with Clover and Gillespie, not to mention half-a-dozen other boys whom I got to know in class and with whom I could talk about books. Edward showed little interest in fortified churches and Border castles. The past did not attract him. For my part, I did not particularly want to hear about his love life, though I think he would have been keen to keep me informed about it. Whatever it may have been, and I think it was both intense and very changeable, it was happening beyond my own areas of activity, especially once I had joined the town Art Club and had adult friends of my own over the river. Much of the time, even in that first year, I never gave him or his family a thought. I always admired his intrepidity and the length he was prepared to go in acts of provocation, and I did my best to push him even further, and he was generally willing to be pushed. But I was more and more engrossed in my work and in my leisure reading, and did not feel the need to be constantly entertained with the adventures of his family. In fact, by the end of that first term he had become more dependent on me than I on him, though I remained grateful for his protection and for his early advice. He could be very good company at most times; we even indulged in a few shared jokes quite outside the family chronicle. We had read *Brave New World* at much the same time and found the references to zippyjams – a convenient form of garment, easy to put on, easier still to take off, like a banana skin – irresistibly funny. I suppose they enabled us to indulge our private sexual fantasies. But even zippyjams could pall, and there often came a time when I felt the need of a change, even of a release. Of course, with the advent of the new regime, and the arrival on the scene of Ferret-Face – to whom we took an instant and, as it turned out, lasting dislike – we became once more a bit closer, the new tyranny providing us with a common enemy, or, rather, with three of them. This was when, in the course of my second year, our partnership started to develop rapidly in ingenuity, in daring and in outrage, though it could only blossom to its full extent in my third year, when I had attained such a degree of privilege in the school hierarchies – and this was indeed a most agreeable victory both over the house and Ferret-Face – that I was placed more or less beyond the reach of any of the accepted forms of punishment, a weakness in the system that we had been quick to spot and that we were to exploit with eager glee and a large measure of impunity.

But part of me always remained outside these childish games. It is a cruel thing to say, but Edward was, for me, little more than a toy to which I would return when I felt the need of excitement or a bit of light relief, or a fit of shared, shaking giggles, the tears running down our cheeks, a time off from working my patient way onto the history side against the wishes of Ferret-Face, or, later, from sitting up swotting for an Oxford award. For myself, Moloch and Medea were little more than joke figures, cut-outs from a comic album; and one could have too much of the best of comic albums. Edward, on the other hand, had always needed a witness to his daring, or to the preposterousness of his family, itself something that was only a joke when it could be shared; someone to impress, and, at the same time, to co-operate with; and, by my second year, he had, for some reason – probably just because I had happened to have been put next to him the year before – assigned that role to myself.

It was almost as if I had not only been the chosen witness, but had actually *created* the Edward of outrage, melodrama and exaggeration. Who, I occasionally wondered, had filled that role before I had arrived on the scene, in his first year in the house? There must have been someone; he would have withered away in the absence of an appreciative audience of at least one. But I never heard him refer to such an essential prop to his personality, to my forerunner; for there could only have been *one* of them, Edward would have needed to have the use of an exclusive court jester. For that matter, he hardly ever referred to the past – save in respect of his parents' separation when he was about ten: I never discovered anything about his preparatory school, even whether it had been in England or in Ireland; and he seldom spoke of his childhood. He seemed to have as little interest in his own past as he did in that of England – or, even more astoundingly, in that of Ireland. He must have been that unique specimen: an Irishman who turned his back on history. I suppose this deliberate amputation – for so it seemed to me at the time – this incompleteness, had something to do with his childlike obsession with the immediate present, the palpable here and now, his grabbing at instant satisfaction and acclaim. There could never be any question of having to wait; every need had to be met on the spot and patience was something quite unknown to him. How many times, later in life, have I seen him explode, stamp and storm, go purple in the face, because he had to wait in a queue! He was completely stuck in the present hour, just as, when I had met him that time in Paris, he had seemed stuck in 1936. The past was something that was over, finished, that was all. He displayed as little interest in the future, and quite failed to understand me when I tried to persuade him that the quickest way of escaping from Hell-Hole, Ferret-Face and his favourites was to work hard so as to earn a place, as quickly as possible, at Oxford or at Cambridge.

4

Gestures and Genuflections

I had come out on the terrace of the British Museum for a break and to have a smoke. A few yards away, I could see the familiar figure of Count Geoffrey Potocki de Montalk, his long greasy hair hanging halfway down his back, and dressed in his dubious, heavily stained red velvet toga that seemed to have been made out of the discarded curtains of a run-down boarding house. He was wearing sandals, though it was February, and his feet looked more than usually dirty, especially between the toes. The Count was holding his usual flag of recognition, *Action Française*, designed to be carried and to be prominently displayed (it was still folded up so as to reveal just its title) rather than to be read; I am not even sure that the Count, who was, of all things, a New Zealander, could read French. I rather hoped that he would not notice me, as I was very short of cigarettes. So I kept well behind him, in the shadow of one of the Grecian columns, while he, like the prow of an old wooden man-of-war, his dirty long hair trailing in the wind, looked ahead, surveying the scene from halfway down the steps.

At this moment, a huge black Daimler, old-fashioned, almost as high as it was long, its brasswork highly polished and shining in the thin February sun, a yellow flag with squares of red and blue fluttering from the bonnet, turned with majestic slowness into the Museum forecourt, circling gracefully, and coming to a gentle halt right at the centre of the flight of steps. The uniformed chauffeur, his collar buttoned up to the top, jumped out, opening the left-hand door, and pulling out a collapsible step. A man in a tail-coat was the first to emerge, leaning forward against the light grey lining of the inside of the door, and advancing his hand to help out a very tall, erect figure, in dove grey, long grey gloves, a grey veil, and carrying a grey reticule, as she stooped expertly to avoid disarranging her grey toque against the roof of the car. The reticule was covered with some silvery material that shimmered in the sun. She stood bolt upright, very straight-backed and tight-waisted, while another lady, in pale mauve, and wearing a flowered hat, climbed out of the car, helped by the man in the tail-coat. The three figures advanced slowly and evenly up the steps, the one in the toque in the middle, the man to her left, the lady to her right, while one of the top-hatted doormen moved down to meet them, holding his hat, with its gold band, in his hand. As an habitué of the Reading Room, I did not need to be told who the lady in the middle was. I had seen her often enough in the Pantiles, Tunbridge Wells. Queen Mary was on one of her regular visits to the Chinese porcelain section of the British Museum.

I moved hurriedly to one side, so as not to be in the way of the small, but impressive, royal procession, as it moved methodically, and in perfect line, up the steps. Unfortunately, the Count who had at once spotted the arrival of his fellow-monarch, now turned round, in order to position himself as near as possible to the middle of the terrace, and, seeing me retreating hurriedly in the direction of one of the pillars, seized me by the sleeve of my sports-coat, holding me tightly with his hand, which was as dirty as his feet. 'Come and salute your sovereign,' he enjoined me, in a ringing voice, raising his right hand (*Action Française* having been temporarily transferred to one of the mysterious folds of his stained toga) in what looked to me like a Fascist salute. As the trio came level with us, the Count called out, in a loud, but I suppose respectful, voice, 'Ave'. The gentleman in tails, his face reddening, and the lady in the flowered hat, looked at the two of us in some surprise, and, I thought, understandable distaste, though I did not see why I should be included in their disapproving glance. But the ramrod lady, advancing majestically as if on hidden

43

wheels beneath her grey fur-trimmed long skirt, looked right through us, as if we had been transparent (I would have done anything to have been transparent during that agonising moment), her very blue eyes betraying no emotion whatsoever, her face, heavily enamelled seen close up, not showing the slightest movement. If she had heard the greeting – as she must have done, for it resounded right across the terrace – her expression registered absolutely nothing. Two more of the top-hatted doormen, bare-headed, had opened up the double-doors – one could not have imagined the toque going through one of the revolving ones, which, in any case, would not have allowed the trio to move forward in line – and the three figures disappeared inside. The visit must have been un-announced, for there was no sign of the Director, generally prominent on these occasions, and giving a series of slight bows as he came down the steps towards the royal party.

The Count seemed especially pleased with his performance, explaining to me that he had greeted his fellow-sovereign in the ancient Roman manner, and asking me why I had remained silent. Had I not wished to salute my sovereign? Was I a republican? A communist? I shook him off as soon as I could, making my way, deeply ashamed of myself, my face still burning, back to my seat in the Reading Room, where at least I would be safe from the Count. Next time, I promised myself, I would be more careful; I would take a look through the revolving doors, before exposing myself out on the terrace. Thinking about the encounter, as I made my way down the long corridor leading to the great circular room, it occurred to me that the Pretender to the Polish Throne had put on the same sort of act of sheer buffoonery, the same exaggerated display of over-elaborate deference, that Edward had often put on, mostly for my benefit, trying to maintain a face meant to indicate a dignified reserve – creases of laughter would sometimes break through round the edges of his eyes – when greeting certain categories of people or certain objects. Poor Edward, I thought; he would have no one to play up to at the present moment, no one to witness one of his most studied displays of quite grovelling greeting. Perhaps that would have been one of the most painful deprivations of his condition at that time, February 1938: no gallery to play to, no one to applaud, no one to laugh at his capacity for wonderful ham-acting, just the usual professional eye, indifferent, unamused, but watchful, at regular intervals, in order to make sure that all was as it should be.

The first time I had seen Edward put on that particular act – mainly, I think, for my benefit, though the person to whom it was ostensibly and most vigorously addressed was also included in it, and was expected to respond with suitable gravity – it had been completely unrehearsed and had been a particularly happy inspiration brought about as the result of a chance encounter. I think even the extra trimmings, like cream on the top of a cake, had been added without forethought. We were out on a Sunday afternoon walk, not a long one, but an easy, gently rambling affair. We had got as far as the already ugly village of Meole Brace on the outskirts of Shrewsbury, and were semi-ambling, semi-swaggering down a street of new council houses in a sickly beige plaster. All at once, one of the front-doors, painted a pale yellow, opened, revealing an untidy-looking woman in straggling dark hair, wearing an apron. She was saying goodbye to a Catholic priest, in a long black cassock, with a line of little buttons, and wearing on his head a biretta – I had never seen one before, but Edward told me what it was called later on. We had passed a little earlier an ugly Catholic church, Turin-style with campanile, painted a pale green, so this may have accounted for the presence of the, to me, strange, even alarming, black-dressed figure, shod in large black boots. Without warning, without even so much as a word or a look in my direction, and to my utter amazement, my companion rushed forward in the direction of the advancing priest and threw himself on the ground on both knees in front of him. I looked on, wondering what on earth Edward would do next. What he did was to seize the startled man's right hand which he proceeded to kiss greedily, as if it had been trifle laced with sherry, making loud sucking noises. The priest, broad-faced and thick-set, abundant dark hair curling around his little biretta, after a start of surprise, or possibly dismay, seemed to adjust himself to this unusual social situation, responding in kind, but with rather more restraint, placing a large red hand on the boy's red curls, and giving him his blessing, or I suppose that was what it was, because the words were murmured, as if not meant to be heard by a standing witness; they may have been in some sort of Latin. For some time, Edward went on clinging to the broad peasant hand, keeping up the succulent mouthing noises, alternating them with a low moaning. What added to the strangeness of the scene presented to me was the fact that Edward was dressed in our Sunday clothing: top-hat, tails, haircord trousers and low waist-coat. The top-hat he had placed, upside-down, on the ground beside him; and his tails were trailing humbly in the dusty road, as if asking forgiveness for such ostentation. The priest eventually disengaged his hand from my friend's avid embrace, rubbing it as he went away, then taking out an enormous handkerchief in red and white check, and wiping it. Edward's performance had been quite splendid, all the more so because it had taken me completely by surprise. As far as I knew, there had been no previous practice. Edward got up off his knees quite slowly and with a sort of calm deliberation, as if a little holiness had been retained in and around his curly head, then started brushing the dust off his striped Sunday trousers at the knees, his face still registering the appearance of an inner piety. It was only when he came alongside me that it began rapidly to dissolve into wave after wave of uncontrollable hilarity, soon transmitted to mine. We made our way back to the school, shaking with laughter. Edward, I thought, had more to him than I had reckoned with.

This spontaneous performance, put on in such totally unsuitable

surroundings – rather as if the Virgin Mary had made an unspon-
sored appearance to a crowd of Saturday shoppers in Bromley High
Street – gave me at least a foretaste of Edward's genuflectionary
capabilities. These were to be given further illustration, this time in a
series of repeat performances of mounting intensity, again beneath
an exterior of studied gravity, during my brief stay with him in
Dublin, a year or so after the Meole Brace 'prostration'. We did a lot
of travelling between the centre of the city, Booterstown, where his
mother lived, and places on the coast, generally on the top of Dublin
Corporation trams. Every time we passed a church – and these were
all uniformly hideous, painted in garish colour washes, and with
appalling-looking plaster saints on the outside – every quarter of a
mile or so, nearly all the passengers on the top deck would cross
themselves, generally discreetly, as if unwilling to be observed, as in
a private act of faith. But this was not Edward's way; on the contrary,
he seemed concerned to outbid the lot of them in an elaborate, not to
say ecstatic, display of intense piety, his eyes raised to the roof of the
tram and showing their whites, even going down on his knees, among
the used tickets and empty packets of Sweet Afton, in the central
corridor, where there was more space, and crossing himself in huge,
slow, sweeping circles, as it were by numbers: one, two, three, four,
five, the movements accelerating with each successive church, convent, monastery, seminary, wayside cross, Catholic hospital, Catholic school; for these were accorded the full treatment. Some secular
buildings got in as well, being offered honorary clerical status,
including, as I remember, *Goggin's Dining Saloons*, on the road to
Dun Laoghaire. On some journeys, he was on and off his knees
pretty well the whole way. It was even worse if he spotted, among the
passengers on the top deck, a priest or a nun, or several of each. Then
his repeated reverences knew no bounds; he would introduce a
verbal accompaniment of low groans and *mea culpas*; and I thought he
was certain to cause himself serious injury, so vigorously did he

throw himself into his manual gyrations which began to involve a similar twisting of his whole torso.

I was not concerned just for him, but started to have fears for my own comfort. Surely, sooner or later, someone would be bound to take offence? I wanted to remove myself from such dangerously compromising company, even thinking of going to sit downstairs. But I stuck it out, being dependent on my friend as to our destination, having no idea where we were going or where to get out. I was the prisoner of my increasingly dangerous companion. But at least I did take care not to be drawn in and not to start imitating him. I could not see myself going through such gesticulations, even in jest, so alien were they to my sensible Low Church upbringing. Besides, I was afraid that, if I attempted to follow his example, I might make mistakes: which hand? Did one start at the top? Or at the chest? Or to the right? Or to the left? Did it go clockwise? Or anti-clockwise? Being left-handed, I would have found it difficult to go through such complicated evolutions with my right. I would be bound to get it wrong; then I would be shown up as an imposter, or a heretic, in the eyes of all the top-deck passengers (and Edward, of course, always insisted on sitting right up in the front, so that he could command a maximum audience). When Edward was really laying it on, providing extra trimmings not normally scheduled in this form of display – beating his breast, so that it would emit a hollow sound, putting out low moans – I would try to dissociate myself physically from him, by sitting slightly to the side, or by ostentatiously opening the *Irish Times* and pretending to be engrossed in its contents, as if I had merely happened to be sitting next to the red-head as he bobbed up and down. I knew perfectly well, of course, that the object of these masquerades was not the deity, but myself, that my presence was, as so often, pushing him on, that the mere fact of my being there would make him bolder and bolder in his extravagances. At the same time, I was highly amused by them, wondering just how far he would have to go and still get away with it. Anyhow, get away with it he did. But I was always relieved to get off the tram, especially when, while doing so, I saw several rows of eyes further back, looking at us with what I took to be intense disapproval. To make matters worse, we were far from being inconspicuous, with boaters on our heads, carrying silver-topped canes, and wearing lavender gloves (Edward made a great show of removing his when engaged in crossing himself) and light grey spats over our black shoes, the rather provocative walking-out dress that we had adopted as appropriate to our first appearance together in the Irish capital, as if to emphasise the silliness of our behaviour and to draw attention to our estimation of ourselves in the role of young bloods.

This was Edward's own show. We were in his country, not mine, and he presumably knew the ropes and just how far he could go. Back at school, I had been much more participatory in what generally turned out to be joint religious exercises. These became more frequent and more daring with the arrival at Shrewsbury School of a new chaplain of marked High Church – not to say popish – inclinations. The Revd A. L. E. Hoskyns-Abrahall was a pale, lugubrious-looking man, with strands of longish, very black hair in a series of cowlicks falling over his forehead. His pallor seemed to offer further evidence of Rome. He had previously been a curate in a naval parish, something that caused me then surprise and puzzlement, for, having early steeped myself in Jane Austen, I had naturally assumed that the Senior Service had always displayed a healthy hostility to Enthusiasm and that it provided the most effective bulwark to sound Low Church doctrine. Perhaps this was why our unctuous cleric, his high-pitched voice suggesting that he was permanently afflicted with tummy trouble, had left the navy to come to us. He marked his arrival by introducing to a most unappreciative, and soon openly restive, congregation, juicy new prayers that seemed to run with treacle, one of which, opening with the invocation: 'O

Iesu, the Master-Carpenter, whose wooden nails . . .', pronounced
in a tone of agonising pain, seemed to be sailing pretty close to the
Romish shores (Iesu, spelt in that baroque manner, seemed to give
the show away). And there was another, equally unfortunate, but for
quite different reasons (relating to the products of Royal Doulton),
beginning with a reference, in the same pained wail, to 'The Golden
Flush of Dawn', an unpromising start to the new day. His services
were soon conducted against an increasing background of shuffling
of feet, coughing and suppressed giggling, while the headmaster, an
utterly reliable Low Church Rugbeian, sat in his high decorated
throne looking more and more thunderous.

This time it was I who took the initiative and set the thing in
motion, drawing Edward in much later, when I had embarked on the
second, and more extravagant stage of the operation, feeling that I
had to have a witness to record, and to spread abroad, its success – as
I hoped – or its (still glorious) failure. A boy in my study, also
curly-haired, his curls a rich golden, had been in the habit of visiting
the chaplain at his flat, over the road from my house, in the evenings;
and he soon brought me back reports of the presence in the cleric's
study of a peculiar, foreign-looking piece of furniture: a chair, the
low-slung seat of which was covered in some mauve or purple
material – probably silk – on very short legs, but with a very high
back, which, after consulting people better acquainted with 'abroad'
than I then was, I managed to identify as a *prie-dieu*. The boy told me
that he would kneel on the chair, his hands holding onto its top, the
chaplain placing a long thin white hand on the head of curls. From
what the boy told me, it seemed clear that the chaplain had been
hearing his confession. I told the head boy about these evening visits
and their probable nature, and he reported the matter to the
headmaster. The Revd Hoskyns-Abrahall was on his way from
Shrewsbury not long after that.

But not before I had launched, in the enthusiastic presence of

Edward, my own two-pronged attack. On the first occasion, we went into town and set up our headquarters in a public telephone box that stood outside the station. I rang the reverend's number, and when I heard his acknowledgment, I enquired, in rather a stern and confident voice: 'Is that the Revd Hoskyns-Abrahall?' The treacly voice replied that it was indeed, asking the name of the caller and the nature of his enquiry. 'I am your employer,' I replied, even more sternly, 'and I am not at all satisfied with your work. A great many complaints have reached me about you. I must warn you that you'll have to pull up your socks. But I'll give you one more chance.' The voice the other end went up several whines, giving signs of extreme irritation – I suppose this sort of thing had not happened in his time with the navy – as well as some bewilderment, and asking me once more who I was. 'I told you before, I am your employer, GOD,'' and rang off. Edward had been able to hear the chaplain's voice crackling faintly, but recognisable, in the receiver. It had come off; the operation had been a complete success, so successful indeed that I decided I could not leave it at that, even if it meant assuming a less exalted alias. We walked back up Pride Hill bubbling over with excitement. I could rely on Edward to publicise the conversation.

The next time, we went to the same phone box and I rang the same number, and again I was lucky enough to get a reply. 'It is about my sermon,' I said. 'I am only coming through briefly; would you please come down to the station and pick me up, so that we can discuss it at your place? I thought self-abuse might be rather suitable, but you may have other suggestions, so let us talk about it over a pot of tea.' Again, he enquired who was calling, and I said, in what I thought was the voice of authority, that it was the Bishop of Matabeleland. To our delight, he said, shortly: 'I'll be down right away.' We could not miss this, even at the risk of being spotted and identified; we were in blue suits, my boater had a black band around it which would mark me out as a sixth-former; Edward's had the house colours: chocolate and

51

gold. Hastily, for there was no time to be lost, we took up our respective positions behind two of the iron columns that supported the enormous neo-Gothic canopy covering the station's forecourt. Being slim, I felt pretty secure behind my column; but I noticed with alarm that one of Edward's broad shoulders was quite visibly protruding from behind his protective cover. I got him to seek out a wider observation post which suggested itself in the form of a tall green edifice containing some electrical equipment and which did indeed give him ample cover. We waited breathlessly. In less than five minutes – he really had been in a hurry, then – the chaplain's large open car, painted green, appeared from the direction of Pride Hill, sweeping in a majestic curve, and stopping right by the main entrance. The chaplain, with a sports coat over the black triangle under his dog-collar, his cowlicks gleaming on his pallid brow, jumped out of the car, looked around in all directions, searching for the bishop. Failing to see him outside the station, he went through the barrier and disappeared in the darkness in the direction of the steps that led up to the platforms, re-emerging a few minutes later. His face was even more pallid than usual, this time, I think, with rage, rather than as a reflection of Romish fervour and excess of woe. He got into his car, slammed the door violently, and drove off, quite fast, without a glance behind him. We had seen the whole thing, save when he had been engulfed in the dark interior of the huge station, from start to finish, I moving rapidly round my protecting pillar in accordance with the reverend's changing, and increasingly rapid positions (speed keeping pace with mounting ill-temper), Edward pretty safe behind his broad screen.

For a minute or two, we remained in hiding, even after the big car had disappeared beyond the brow of the steep hill, at the level of the old school. We hardly dared trust our luck; there was always the possibility that he might suddenly double back in his tracks, or approach the station from a different angle in the hope of catching the hoaxers (any schoolmaster would know that these things were generally done in pairs), exposed out in the open. But this was to give him credit for too much guile. It was clear that he was quite unused to the tricks of schoolboys: any other master would have displayed a waiting cunning, in the knowledge that we would be bound to break cover once the visible danger was out of sight. Not so the Revd Hoskyns-Abrahall; he had been properly had. Then we came out into the open forecourt, quite beside ourselves with delight. I had pulled it off a second time. My companion, as we walked back up the hill, *I* still bathed in a sense of triumph, looked at me covertly, with a sort of amazed admiration, and perhaps a little envy.

I suppose we must have told quite a lot of people about my successful impersonation both of God and his lieutenant, the Bishop of Matabeleland, for it soon went right round the school. I was even asked about it in my form; and soon, as is nearly always the case in a closed, inbred community, given the natural tendency of boys cooped up in boarding-schools to exaggerate and to embroider, it rapidly acquired quite inflated proportions. I was credited with further remarks in the course of the first, and brief, telephone conversation; many further episodes were now tagged on, as the whole thing acquired a vastly extended existence over the years, long after I had left the place, as part of schoolboy folklore. It certainly had an amazingly long run, picking up more and more bits along the way. Many years later – nearly thirty, in fact – a healthy-looking, sandy-haired man with very benevolent, but observant blue eyes came into my room at Balliol during my first few days in the college. I thought the pleasant, yet powerful face vaguely familiar, but I could not put a name to it there and then. 'You won't remember me,' he said, in order to explain his presence, 'but I taught you at Shrewsbury.' And, at once, the intervening years fell away; I was once more a schoolboy. The face had hardly changed at all; it was that of the Revd Frank MacCarthy, who had attempted to teach me biology and had had rather more success teaching me divinity: an entirely safe Low-Churchman, recruited, I think, by the headmaster, H. H. Hardy, in the knowledge that there could have been no greater contrast, in terms of temperament, manner of delivery, theology, and understanding of boys, to the departing Hoskyns-Abrahall. I told him that of course I remembered him, he hadn't changed a bit. 'I remember you,' he replied, his very blue eyes sparkling with mirth, 'you were the boy who phoned up that pompous ass, Hoskyns-Abrahall, telling him that you were his employer, in other words, God'; or he thought it might have been the other way round, that I had opened with the words: 'God speaking' – there were several versions current at the time in the Masters' Common Room. He did not seem a bit shocked by such blasphemy, finding it, on the contrary, a really good joke, the recollection of which still brought broad smiles to his extremely wise face. He knew about the Bishop of Matabeleland, too; that had also gone the rounds among the staff. There did not seem to have been much solidarity among the clergy on the site. He went on to tell me – with added amusement – that if I had once masqueraded as a bishop, the disgraced chaplain had become a real one some time after his departure from Shrewsbury. He was now, he concluded, chuckling, the Bishop of Lancaster – with *Black*pool (his voice went down as he emphasised the first syllable, as if there were something comical or slightly improper about the place) in his diocese. He thought that particularly suitable; it would give full scope to Hoskyns' skill at conjuring tricks, at bowing and scraping; perhaps he might even perform in open-air services on the promenade or on the beach. He added that he was Higher than ever.

The God-Speaking-from-the-Phone-Booth episode and its follow-up naturally put Edward on his mettle. He would have to do something about it, if he were going to retrieve his reputation even in his own eyes as well as in the house at large (his fame had not as yet extended to the school – he had made no friends there, as far as I knew – but this he was going to remedy). I soon learnt what his plan of action was to be. Religion would once more offer him his preferred stage. He informed me, with gravity, as if it were a state secret, one weekday, that on the following Sunday he would stage a faint towards the end of the evening service in the school chapel and that he would then be carried out. I had my doubts about the whole thing – it was surely rather difficult to faint to order – but I kept these to myself, merely expressing the hope that those to each side of him in his pew would not be small, puny boys, but two of his own build. Actually, I did not think he would go through with it; he would either get cold feet at the last moment, or give the game away by succumbing to a fit of the giggles, before, or while, being carried out; and, as he sat near the front, there would be a long way to go. I suppose he had thought of that, too; he would get a maximum audience that way, as he had with the tramcar performances. By the end of the week, with other things on my mind, I had quite forgotten about his intended gesture, and was thus as much taken by surprise as the rest of the congregation when, in the course of the sermon, there was a loud clatter, followed by a crash, from up near the front of the chapel. The preacher halted in mid-sentence. Some of the boys further back stood up to see what was happening. There was a pause and an agonised silence, and then, after much pushing and shoving among black tail-coated backs towards the front, the large figure of Edward appeared in the aisle, supported under the armpits by two hefty-looking boys; his body, far from being stiff, lolled about in all directions, like that of a broken doll, his feet dragging along on the black and white tiled floor. His eyes were shut and his face looked quite pallid. There was complete silence, save for the sound of his dragging feet, as he was carried from the building, and it was only after the door of the chapel had been banged shut that people started to sit down. Even the headmaster looked quite startled for a moment. Then the preacher started up again, and, after a few minutes, the two

55

large boys reappeared in the aisle and made their way back to their seats. I had to admit that it had been a star performance. I learnt later that Edward had been carried to the house on a stretcher and that he had been put in the sick bay for observation.

He reappeared later on the next day, after the school doctor had had a look at him. He thought it must have been the heat. He accepted the many anxious enquiries about how he felt with his usual polite good grace. He was perfectly all right now. But, once we were alone together, he could hardly contain himself. He was not the sort of person to be content with a silent triumph; and, as I was the only person to have had foreknowledge of the planned faint, I was expected to express my admiration for the skill and realism with which he had carried it off. This I had to concede; but I still thought that the whole thing had been rather silly. What had it proved? Merely that he had gone through with something when he had said he would. What good had it done? Chapel was not hostile terrain; on the contrary, it was something of a compensation for the philistinism of the house. The pretend faint had not been a blow against the system; Hoskyns-Abrahall had been sent packing. The preacher that evening had been a pleasant, kindly, if slightly dotty old clergyman. He had caused a lot of inconvenience, embarrassment and physical exertion to his two completely unknown neighbours; and, even from his own point of view, he was denied the opportunity to savour the success of the operation to the full. I had been the only person to have been let in on the secret of it in advance, so I alone could be allowed to share in the satisfaction in something efficiently and convincingly carried out. He could not very well put it out abroad that it had been a put-up job, a Sunday evening hoax.

I was finding plenty of other things to engage my curiosity; I was deriving, with each successive term, more and more satisfaction from my work, more and more enjoyment in the company of my history master and my fellow-historians. Often, even when we were fairly close, I would have been hard put to say how Edward spent his spare time, save that it often seemed to weigh rather heavily on him. I think he was keen on golf, but I don't know whether he was given the possibility of playing it while at school. What he did with his leisure was something of a mystery to me; I did not really want to know. But I was not prepared to play his full-time partner in an English version of *Les Enfants Terribles*.

In fact I managed to opt out more and more. For instance, I avoided but he put himself down for a week-end at the Shrewsbury School Boys' Club – or Mission – in some unpleasant area of Liverpool. It seemed an odd choice. He would have been quite incapable of making any sort of contact at all with the tough working-class boys who were drawn into this no doubt worthy enterprise, and I could imagine how his nose would turn up in distaste when confronted with the powerful odour of sweat and socks in the gymnasium or during an energetic game of basketball. Yet he came back from this visit very pleased with himself. Apparently, he had caused havoc from start to finish. He had been rude to some poor well-meaning curate who spent a lot of his spare time with the boys of the Mission; he had refused to participate in any of the group activities; and his major achievement had been to create an enormous traffic jam somewhere right in the centre of Liverpool. He had been travelling (once again) on the top deck of a tram which he had succeeded in immobilising by pulling down the long steel arm which connected the tram to the overhead electric wire that supplied the current. The school party had been over an hour late in getting to the Mission. He had thought this a tremendous joke.

It was much the same when he volunteered, the year that Hitler came to power, for the Duke of York's Camp, held every summer somewhere on the East Coast. He told me about it some time later; for, as I recently learnt, he had only spent a day and three-quarters in the camp. The first evening, when they had all been sitting cross-legged round the big camp fire, the Duke himself in the middle and wearing shorts, he had contented himself with singing his own private versions of the jolly songs (accompanied by gestures, the clapping of heads, the clapping of knees, and so on) that concluded each day of these worthy inter-class efforts. But no one had been able to hear the no doubt derisive words that he had been using, so this particular piece of sabotage would appear to have fallen rather flat, or so it seemed to me, when he told me about it. His achievement on this occasion had been purely negative. The Duke of York's Camp had got him out of the OTC manoeuvres at Strensall. I don't suppose, with all the crowd that would have been milling around on such collective occasions, he would even have been much noticed, much less heard and listened to. I expect all he had actually done there, during his very short stay (so suddenly interrupted, I was to learn, thanks to my intervention), was to have got by, with a minimum of effort, keeping well out of the way when there had been any fetching or carrying to be done. I could have imagined nothing more improbable than the sight of Edward ladling out soup with a big wooden spoon to keen-looking boys as they queued up, in shorts and bare-chested, and he would have been always somewhere else when there had been any call for volunteers. Even in a terrain so unfavourable, and where everyone could be accounted for at any given time, he would have nosed out some quiet corner where he could get through the day unobserved, and with the added satisfaction that he was avoiding some strenuous expedition or a round of volley-ball on the beach. As far as I could make out, it had been more a matter of avoidance, of keeping his head down, than sabotage.

Later, when we went to London together he or I – or both of us – decided to call at King Street, Covent Garden. I cannot remember whether either of us joined the Young Communist League, but Edward certainly obtained a number of ill-printed, lurid Soviet posters, depicting muscle-bound male and female workers, the former in caps, the latter in head-scarves, marching radiantly towards the golden future. These he then put up in his study, in the hope I think that they would provoke Ferret-Face; but the housemaster failed to comment on their presence. He seemed not even to have *seen* them, and the boys in his study preferred coloured pictures of semi-nude girls to posters of athletic-looking Stalinists with little sex appeal, staring eyes, and idiotic expressions.

5

The Raven

In the normal course of events, we would probably have drifted completely apart, and this would have turned out very much to my own benefit. As for Edward, I don't think it would have made very much difference; he would have gone on in his own way, whether in my company, or on his own. More likely, he would soon have acquired – as I believe he did, later on – another more amenable, more easily impressed *compagnon de route*, one who would allow him first place, and would be prepared to give him full-time attention and attendance; something I had never been willing to offer. But, some time in my third year at school, something happened that brought the two of us together again. Medea had allowed herself to be expected on several successive speech days, and, each time, Edward had worked himself up into excited expectation of what might ensue, as a result of her presence, and my meeting her. But, on each occasion, she had called the visit off at the last moment, perhaps having had confirmation that Moloch too had decided not to come over. But, quite without warning, and on some private impulse, she took advantage of a half-term holiday some time in the winter to pay a brief visit to Shrewsbury; and, like everything else she undertook, she had to do it in style. So she took a room at the Raven Hotel, asking Edward to bring me along to lunch with her there on the Saturday.

For once Edward had not exaggerated. She could put on the charm all right, when it suited her purpose. From the moment I met her, for a drink before lunch, she made a great fuss of me, while, at the same time, using me as an object through which to make

6

unfavourable comparisons as far as Edward was concerned. How nice it was of me to have given so much of my time to her son! Perhaps he might even draw some benefit from the company of a boy far more intelligent – yes, she had heard excellent reports of my progress in school from my masters (I knew perfectly well that she had never met any of them) – and more assiduous than Edward. I might even manage to teach him a modicum of manners and to show some consideration for others. She could see at once that I had been well brought up; she would so like to meet my parents. Perhaps it would be possible some time? She went on to say that generally she had disapproved of Edward's friends and associates; they had been the sort of people who, being as idle and as ill-organised as himself, he would be likely to go for: birds of a feather. I must have noticed that he liked to see his own shortcomings mirrored in those with whom he went around. But this time she had real hopes of improvement – well, perhaps not that, Edward was not going to change, it was already too late. But it looked to her as if I might even then have some influence on him for the good. What was I most interested in? What did I read? Who were my favourite authors? Hardy, oh yes, of course Edward could not be induced to read that sort of thing, much too deep, and he had such a shallow mind, though she had always tried to put him in the way of good books. Maybe, coming from *me* – for anything *she* had to suggest would be like water off a duck's back – he might listen. She had tried and tried, all her friends knew how hard she had tried, but it had been quite useless. One of the reasons that, again and again, she had decided not to come over for speech day was the knowledge that she would only hear bad reports of him: no progress in class, no aptitude for sport, no team spirit, no consideration for other people, rudeness to his superiors. She had sometimes hoped – wrongly of course – that with good examples around him, there might be some improvement in his behaviour; but he had always let her down, almost as if it had been on purpose.

On and on she went, though she still managed to put down a plentiful supply of food and drink in between this chronicle of woe. Could I put myself in the position of a mother? I thought that I would find this rather difficult, but she did not expect an answer; and she went on, appealing to me for understanding and help. She really looked as if she meant it, as if she already knew that she could count on me as an ally. I was so much more *mature* than Edward; she had noticed that right away, from the very moment I had come into the room.

Edward had been right in two things: his mother had enormous charm, and she was still very good-looking, with a fine head of thick reddish-brown hair, well-shaped eyebrows of the same colouring, and with very blue eyes, though with a tendency to water. Her complexion was uneven; there were patches of a darker red, and some of her veins stood out. But she was soberly dressed, had a most agreeable manner, as if genuinely pleased to have had the opportunity of meeting me, and it was from her that Edward had inherited his pleasant, very considerate voice.

She kept up a barrage of compliments and appeals for my collaboration, accepting me at once into her intimacy, as if there was already an understanding between us ('I can see we see eye to eye'), while, at the same time, excluding her son from any direct participation in the conversation, as if he were deaf and dumb or an idiot, while making comparisons that were so many overt references to his inadequacies.

She kept this up all through lunch, which was an excellent one. Perhaps what surprised me most was the attitude adopted by Edward. He quite refused to be drawn in, as if the conversation did not concern him, and his mother had been talking about someone he had never heard of. Or perhaps the tune was so familiar that he had acquired the knack of switching it off at will. Anyhow, during the early stages of the meal he looked about him, his eyes ranging over the other people who were having lunch, many of them parents feeding up their little boys, assessing his surroundings, which were indeed luxurious, at least in the eyes of a denizen of our house. He seemed to be examining the lights that hung in bright clusters from the ceiling, or taking in the uniforms – peach-coloured – of the little messenger-boys, rushing around busily under their round caps, carrying silver trays. Whatever it was that was claiming his attention, he appeared fully engrossed, as if unaware of the course of the conversation going on around him. Never for a moment did his eyes stray in the direction of his mother's patchy, mottled face. He was present: quiet, unassuming, well-behaved, attentive to our needs, passing the cruet or the butter, refilling our glasses; and yet he was absent, as if plunged in other concerns. Occasionally, his eyes would catch mine, as I listened to his mother's flow, with a suggestion of shared amusement, as if to say: Well, did I not tell you? But mostly, when he was not looking casually round the room, occasionally cocking an ear to pick up a fragment of conversation coming from a nearby table, he would keep his head down in the direction of his plate. He certainly ate with remarkable appetite, taking care to have a second helping of each course, compensating for Ferret-Face's meagre board. He would at least get that much out of Medea. She had invited me, partly to win me over, but also to use me as a means of provoking her son. But he quite refused to be provoked, looking quite unconcerned throughout the meal, smiling every now and then at some private joke or at some happy thought that had just occurred to him.

His self-control was as admirable as it was unfamiliar. His mother and he, though avoiding ever addressing each other directly, were clearly engaged in a game familiar to both of them, and in which each had acquired considerable skills. He let the conversation flow on around him as if it had been the murmur of a running brook. I knew that I had not said anything that might have impressed his mother –

she would in any case have been very difficult to impress, her ignorance being so enormous as to remove her from even the awareness of anything that could have been seen as impressive – and that I was being used as an instrument in what was clearly yet another chapter in a long-drawn-out engagement between the two of them. I was quite flattered by her profession of interest in what I was doing: where I would go after leaving school, where I lived, whether I had brothers and sisters, what my father's profession had been, adding more than once how much she would like to meet my parents some time. Dublin was such a small place, one so seldom met interesting people, she was quite provincial herself; how could she help not being?

But I was not taken in. I thought she was cunning, in a sly sort of way, as well as ingratiating; she was far too anxious to please, and was the sort of person to inspire lack of confidence from the moment of first meeting. She also seemed rather cruel. I sensed that Edward and she were engaged in a dialogue which, while never being direct, followed certain accepted rules understood only by the pair of them. Although she made a point of talking only to me, I felt I was an eavesdropper on a coded conversation reserved to the two of them. There was no doubt a great deal of mutual dislike – to put it mildly – in their relationship; but it was also something of which they both stood in need. I understood on this very first encounter that mother and son were prisoners of each other, and that, however much they detested one another – he really did think of her as a monster, she really did regard him as a hopeless dolt who would never achieve anything – they were still unable to disengage from a running fight, sometimes frontal, more often oblique and rather dirty, that, as soon as they were alone together, took up much of their time and most of their energies. I could understand that Edward, at least, was grateful for my presence, as it delayed the outbreak of hostilities until such time as they were once more alone together.

On this occasion – a memorable one, for so much followed from it – I could not but admire my friend's forebearance in the face of such a running barrage of disagreeable allusions and petty stings, lobbed apparently in my direction, but meant to be caught halfway across the net by the player in the middle: a verbal tennis as unorthodox as everything about the relationship between this oddly self-completing pair. I would not previously have thought him capable of thus holding his fire, keeping his head down, and retaining a cool, even good-humoured detachment. It was clear that he had discovered the most effective weapon with which to parry her relentless – and, in fact, self-defeating – provocation. As on a few other occasions, I had to admit that there was more in him than I had suspected: an immense, powerful, and, indeed, infuriating fund of patience, unruffled calm (at least on the surface), the appearance of a polite indifference, the ability to retain his good manners, even while being subjected to a very alert, if not very intelligently inspired or cleverly conducted, malevolence.

I was not in the least fooled by his mother; her wiles were too patently obvious. I realised that I was only the latest pawn in a long-running operation, conducted, with uncharacteristic energy (as I was later to discover, she was anything but energetic, spending every afternoon lying down on her bed), against her son, or, rather, the only one who had remained within her reach, my friend's elder brother having years previously had the good sense to remove himself, I think to Australia. I thought she was unpleasant, as well as crudely over-dramatic, a ham actress who had attained a sort of professional perfection in sheer badness of performance. She would not even have made a good clown, for she had no sense of fantasy, and her imagination was limited and banal. She was very easy to see through. What I retained most from that first meeting was that Edward had a great deal to put up with. For while life with Medea might be amusing to talk about from the safe distance of Shrewsbury (so that even the house had something to offer, as far as this embattled adolescent was concerned), it was anything but fun to be lived in reality, in daily contact. It struck me too that, in the always tense relations with his mother, Edward had schooled himself, no doubt from bitter experience, to achieve a degree of serenity that must have been quite infuriating to her, fuelling the impotence of her rage. I concluded from this first, but quite convincing experience, that the best thing that could ever happen to him would be if, following the example of his brother, he could get clear away from his mother, make a complete break, never return to Dublin, forget about her, and thus get on with his own life unimpeded and removed from her baleful influence. But, of course, this was a facile judgment; she was his mother, not, thank goodness, mine; there may even have been some measure of affection between them. How was I to know? A bad mother for anyone, is what I thought at the time, on leaving the Raven after that excellent lunch.

Booterstown

It had been decided at the lunch that Edward's mother would come to the speech day in the following summer and that I would introduce her to my parents, with a view to arranging for Edward to spend a fortnight at my home in Tunbridge Wells and for me then to follow on, later in the summer, and stay at her house in Dublin for a fortnight. I did not much relish the prospect of having Edward on my hands at home for a fortnight. I did not know how to keep him occupied, and Tunbridge Wells was a place I had never felt much like sharing with anyone, even my best friend; I had grown accustomed to keeping it to myself. And I was none too keen to stay with his mother; but the idea of visiting, for the first time, a foreign country quite outweighed these considerations.

So, in the summer, my parents were introduced to her, my father being quite captivated by the red-haired lady's effusive charm, though my mother was later to claim that she had never been taken in for a moment: she had met that type before, they were totally unreliable, that was the thing about the Irish. But they too had seemed to get on quite well at the time. All I can remember about the speech day is that Edward and I were unceremoniously slung out of the OTC tent, to which we had introduced ourselves in order to obtain refreshments, by the commandant of the Corps, Major West, the school's leading militarist. We had both been expelled from the Corps earlier in the year.

Edward's stay in Tunbridge Wells was uneventful. He was very much on his good behaviour, charming both my parents and my mother's bridge friends by his perfect manners. He seemed to be constantly in attendance, rushing forward to open doors, taking coats, advancing chairs, even helping with the washing-up in the evenings. My mother annoyed me by frequently remarking on how well brought up my friend was, so unlike the rather uncouth Clover. Perhaps Edward might be a good example to me. Later, she was to revise this good opinion, stating that there had been more smarm than charm. But at the time he had gone down very well with everyone. He had listened to my father's stories, laughing at the right places; and he really seemed to like my mother. I could not help feeling that he was laying it on rather thick, in order to put me, by contrast, in a bad light. But I think this was unfair; he was naturally polite and genuinely deferential. Apart from a piece of wanton vandalism, in which we were interrupted before we had had time to do much damage, in the little churchyard at Bidborough, we behaved reasonably well, perhaps because there was no one to impress.

We went to Mereworth, beyond Hadlow, for a day, to visit the vicar and his wife, who had been a schoolfriend of Edward's mother. Their son, Chrissie Mayne, was at the time head of the school. Shortly after leaving Shrewsbury, he was murdered at a Soho party, and his body, covered in stab wounds, was later retrieved from the Thames. Edward's mother did not appear to bring much luck to anyone with whom she had, at one time or another, been closely associated.

When my fortnight in Ireland was due, I took the mailboat from Holyhead. My first sight of the Free State – as it still was – was the slogan painted in large white letters on the jetty at Dun Laoghaire: BOYCOTT BRITISH GOODS. I mentioned this to Edward, when he met me at the landing-stage; he seemed amused by it. I think we took a little train to Booterstown, to his mother's house. During the first few days of my stay, she made a great fuss of me; nothing could be too much trouble. At the same time, she left us very much to our own devices. Edward proved an assiduous and most considerate guide, taking me to the crypt of St Michan's, to the Castle (an old man there told us about hearing the banshees just before the death of some leading figure), Phoenix Park, Blackrock, Dalkey and Greystones. We were invited to a party at a big white house somewhere on the coast; our hostess was Madame Starkie – for so she was addressed, though she did not appear to be in the same category as Edward's aunt, the pious novelist, Madame Roussel. Madame Starkie, whose husband, Walter was professor of Romance Languages at Trinity College, was Italian, and rather frightening. The Starkies seemed to know everyone, even asking me if I would like to meet Mr de Valera. Well, of course I would. So it was arranged. It seemed very easy to meet people in Dublin. I was most impressed. On the way back, we were in an open car, Edward driving, which he did much too fast for my comfort. We were going along a white road; on the verge, walking towards the car, there was a girl in a red dress, with very dark, long hair and a pale face. She smiled at us. It was the first time I had ever *looked* at a girl. I thought she was very beautiful and rather exotic.

Edward and I also went to see an English cat burglar who was being held in the local police station. He was a most engaging cockney who seemed to have established very friendly relations with the *gardai*. He told us that he had found London rather hot for him and had crossed over to try his luck in Booterstown. He had cleared out most of St Helen's Road, before his luck ran out. I learnt later from Edward that his mother had put in a claim for a fur coat which she said had been stolen from her house; but it turned out that not only had her house, No. 23, not been burgled, but that she did not possess a fur coat. It was much about this time that she was also in trouble with the people who ran the Irish Sweepstake, for whom she acted as an agent when on her visits to England. There had been talk of fraud, which had all been hushed up. But they sacked her from the Sweep.

She told me how cruel her husband had been to her when she was still a defenceless young woman. The man was a brute; he used to beat her. She added that when she had left his house to seek safety elsewhere, he had refused to let her take her silver. I thought this very disgraceful and, rather taken with the boldness of the suggestion, I volunteered to get it back for her. It seemed to me that, as a visitor, I had nothing to lose. She gave me a detailed account of all the objects that belonged to her and where they would be placed in the doctor's drawing-room. There seemed no reason to delay this attempt to put matters right; we both agreed that we would get her silver back on the very next day. Edward knew the habits of the household, as well as his father's visiting hours. We would go there when he was on his rounds; Edward would engage his aunt, who acted as his father's housekeeper, in conversation, while I waited in the coal-cellar. When the way was clear, he would give the signal, by stamping on the floor; then all I had to do was to make for the drawing-room and fill a large cloth bag provided by his mother with her silver, and then make off through the garden, climb the wall at the back, and jump on the first tram that came along (the house was on a main road). Edward would follow on in due course, keeping his aunt in her sitting-room till I had completed my part in the proceedings. It seemed an excellent plan, and all three of us were most excited by it. Edward even fished out a long-peaked old cloth cap in loud checks, saying that I was to wear it well over my face, to prevent me from being recognised, in case things went wrong. The cloth cap added a spice of danger to the whole enterprise.

We spent much of the evening planning the details of the operation for the following afternoon. It was agreed that Edward and I should travel together on a tram to the stop nearest his father's large house. He would then go in ahead of me, while I made my way, with cloth cap and swagger bag, over the garden wall at the back. He told me where the entrance to the coal-cellar was. Once inside, I should wait in the dark till he gave the signal for me to make my way quickly upstairs – I had to go past the aunt's sitting-room, but he would have a record on very loud, and she was a bit deaf anyway; the drawing-room was at the end of the corridor. I would have to make my way back along the same corridor, then down into the garden and back over the wall, making sure there was no one in the street. I had never been given this sort of assignment in Tunbridge Wells. There was no doubt that things were rather different in the Free State and Dublin seemed to be a place where things happened. I could hardly sleep in my excitement.

The afternoon of the following day we left the house in the highest spirits, Edward's mother accompanying us to the front door and standing waving to wish us good luck, while we waited at the tram stop. Everything went off as planned; there was no doubt that Edward had thought it all out. I waited till he had disappeared through the front door of the large white house, an address, I think, in Lexham Gardens, in a fashionable area of Dublin, a wide street full of doctors' plates. I got over the wall unnoticed from the street, hiding at the back of the coal-cellar behind a tall pile of coal. I could hear Edward's loud, confident voice coming from the room above; he had evidently succeeded in cornering and immobilising his aunt, and soon there was the sound of music, played very loud. All I had to do now was to wait for the signal. I pulled the cap well over my eyes. I had only been in the cellar a few minutes and my eyes were just getting used to the semi-darkness, so that I could make out the vague outlines of objects, when a very young, very small maid came down, carrying a scuttle and an electric torch. The light from the torch threw my cloth-capped shadow in dark silhouette against the far wall, making me look like a giant and elongating the sinister-looking cap. The girl started screaming 'Jesus-Mary, there's a strange man down there', and bolted up the stairs to get help. Edward and his aunt both heard the screams at the same time, though he tried to drown them by turning up the music. Then the maid herself, shaking with terror, presented herself in the sitting-room. I rushed for the entrance of the cellar, scorched across the long garden and over the wall, abandoning both cap and bag on the lawn. Luckily a tram came by almost at once and I jumped on it while it was moving, still sweating from fright. I stayed on the tram as far as the terminus; it seemed best to get as far away as possible from the centre of the city. Then, asking passers-by how to get to Booterstown, I made my dejected way back to No. 23.

Medea had only to take one look at me, capless, bagless and still breathless, to realise that the master-plan had failed hopelessly. She was not in the least bit sympathetic, would not listen to my explanations about the sudden arrival of the maid, and got very angry, saying it was typical of Edward thus to have mismanaged the whole thing. He should have known about the maid; there had always been one. Edward was just a hopeless bungler, and I was no better. How wrong it had been of her to have trusted two silly boys with a grown-up operation (Medea's word for what in fact would have been a burglary); she should have known they would make a hash of it. I tried to point out that the arrival of the maid had not been my fault – it was one of those imponderables that might defeat the best thought-out operation – but she would not hear me out.

Edward arrived about an hour later, having had some difficulty calming down his aunt and persuading her not to ring the police. Even so, the cap and the bag had been found. The former, an old one of Edward's, had been recognised. The aunt was no fool; he was pretty sure that she would have realised what had been afoot. Moreover, she and her brother had found out – I don't know how, though the doctor had long been in the habit of putting private detectives to keep a watch on his estranged wife's house – that Edward had a schoolfriend over from England and staying at St Helen's Road. It would not have been very difficult for them to have identified the be-capped intruder. In short, as he saw it, things

72

looked pretty black. Nor would this be the end of it. At this, his mother started shouting at him, saying that we had got her into an impossible situation. She would be blamed; Charlie (her husband) always blamed her for everything, whereas, from the start, she had been against the whole mad escapade. She then turned on me; it had all been *my* idea. Edward would not have thought of it on his own. She had apparently quite forgotten (she had a highly adjustable memory) that it was she who had first brought up the subject of her sequestrated silver. She went on to say that she should have known better than to have had me to her house (with her usual proneness to verbal inflation, she referred to the little detached place in beige pebble stucco with a tiny front garden and a long, narrow, unkempt back one with a toolshed at the far end, as if it had been a stately Georgian home in the wilds of Co. Wicklow). She would write forthwith to my parents and let them know how I had behaved, how I had betrayed her hospitality. And she then proceeded to assign to me a role that was to become my signature tune in the months to come, indeed for almost two years. I was an evil influence (she talked in gaudy penny postcard clichés that probably had something to do with her convent school education), and I had misled her son from the moment I had met him; she had noticed the change in him at once. It was I who had put him up to things. He had been such a gentle, loving boy (she actually managed to summon up large tears in her very blue eyes at this point) till I had appeared on the scene. I had deliberately turned him against her. It had been a bad day when I had gone to Shrewsbury (she chose to forget that it was she who had insisted on Edward's going there first).

Edward remained silent, making no effort to put in a word for me during this slushy tirade. There was some general law operating here; I was to encounter its effects many times later in life, indeed every time I was to get involved in the affairs of someone else's family; it always ended up in the formation of a family 'popular front' against the intruder, the person from outside. I would not have been surprised if I had not been the instrument of at least a temporary reconciliation, or at least of a brief truce, between mother and son. I had seen such things happen before when I had been at my second preparatory school.

From that day on, things went from bad to worse. The next day, after her rest – she was always at her worst at this time of the afternoon, as if the rest up in her bedroom had merely had the effect of augmenting her cloying self-pity and her aggressiveness – she started on Edward. Some of it I had already heard, for it was part of the daily four o'clock dirge: no one appreciated her; she had never been given a proper chance to develop her talents; had been sent to rotten schools (there seemed little doubt of that); now she was all alone in the world; her husband was a cruel brute who starved her of money and had her spied upon. He was selfish, he had a mistress; the *gardai* and the detective-inspector had made unjust accusations against her in order to blacken her reputation, which was as spotless as driven snow – an unlikely phenomenon in St Helen's Road and no doubt another convent cliché; her son did not care for her; the best thing she could do would be to drive herself into the Liffey and make an end of it. This had always been the cue – they had learnt their parts in this bad play quite by heart – for Edward to intervene, in his politest, most considerate voice: 'But, mother, leave the car first on the quayside; there is no need to take it with you. All you have to do is to jump in' – a remark that later became quite a key phrase in our letters to each other. Why waste the car, after all? It was only a Baby Austin, but still . . . We thought it very funny, and I suppose it was, in terms of schoolboy jokes.

But she did not think it at all funny on this occasion when, switching quite suddenly from the usual whining and lachrymose appeals for pity, sympathy and understanding, she turned to violent action. She was about to pour out the tea. Instead, she hurled the full teapot across the room, in the direction of Edward's head; it was quite a good, very powerful shot, but it just missed him, shattering against a corner of the mantelpiece, spraying hot tea and tea leaves all over the wallpaper above the shelf and smashing some pretty china figurines below the mirror. This was only the opening shot in a vigorous and indeed rather joyous exchange of fire. Edward went with quiet deliberation into the kitchen to put on another kettle, and having, with care, poured himself out a fresh cup of tea, he came back unhurriedly into the room and threw the contents of his full cup over his mother's face which, under the impact of Earl Grey became even more blotched than usual. It was the solemn slowness of his movements that most impressed me, giving to the exchange a sort of religious gravity. Soon, all sorts of objects were hurtling across the drawing-room: the sugar, the sugar-tongs, a jug of cream, a pot of strawberry jam, then one of gooseberry jam, a bottle of ink, a plant in a bowl, a vase with the flowers in it. The fire was so heavily and skilfully sustained on both sides that it was clear that this was not a first performance, that both parties knew the form, and that a great deal of previous practice had gone into perfecting the act. I had noticed, on my arrival, that there were wide stains like huge stars on the wallpaper of both drawing-room and dining-room and that blotches in the hall seemed to offer evidence of the occasional opening out of a second front; but I had thought nothing of them at the time, putting them down to Medea's natural untidiness and to Hibernian national sluttishness. I watched with amazement, and a sort of admiration, taking great delight in the regular sound of smashing. The place soon looked like a battlefield; the walls and floor were awash. After a few more exchanges – including some large books (designed no doubt for the purpose, certainly not to be read: I never saw Medea open a book) – during which no words was spoken by either of the participants, all their attention being on the game, there was an informal truce, ammunition having run out (though I had rather hoped that they would start on the furniture). Edward said to me: 'Let's get out of here and leave her to it.' And we left her amidst the wreckage of the smashed china, the walls spattered with tea, ink, mustard, jams in several colours and consistencies, and some indefinable reddish liquid.

As we left the room – Medea sitting on the floor, her red hair hanging down her face and shoulders in damp and sploshy strands, and surrounded by mostly unidentifiable débris – and went out of the front door, Edward, up till then as calm, as grave and as deliberate as ever, all at once started shaking with laughter. He commented, between hiccoughs, his eyes running with tears of hilarity, that it had been something of a bumper performance, even by his mother's histrionic standards. There had been new additions, unrehearsed flourishes and extra acts. He thought that they might have been provided for my benefit; I was quite sure that this had been the case, though why his mother, who had more or less cast me out morally – and was about to do so physically – should have wanted to play to my gallery I could not make out. It seemed more likely that they had been concerned to outperform one another, under the stimulus of the presence of an outsider. I had been the unwitting accelerator and the inspiration of the new frills to an already well-established 'tea ceremony' – if those were the right words for an exercise in which no tea was actually drunk or eaten, but only thrown. Of course, they could do without me. It was very evident, as I have said, that there had been regular previous lunch and dinner ceremonies (breakfast ones were out, as Medea had hers in bed, brought up by the daily). It was quite clear from his jaunty manner that Edward was pleased that I had been a spectator at the drawing-room scene. I had to admit to myself that it had been quite unlike any of the many quiet and pleasant tea-parties I had attended in Tunbridge Wells, in The Hythe (my grandparents' home in Colchester), or with townspeople in Shrewsbury. So Edward must have felt that he had proved his point. I could report back that all the claims that he had made for Moloch, Medea and the rest of them, back in the house, had been fully justified and that he really did have a pretty amazing family. He remained in excellent spirits for the rest of the day, even to the point of being physically energetic.

He seemed anxious to shake off the cloying atmosphere of St Helen's Road, as if he had wanted to open all the windows of that stuffy, over-furnished – though, on current showing, it would soon be under-furnished, even unfurnished – little house. The sheer vigour and momentum of the piece of bad theatre that I had just witnessed – and, indeed, enjoyed, because of the sound of breakage – might have been ascribed to a deliberate, rather desperate effort to challenge the inescapable suburban banality, the ordinariness of the house, the street and their neighbourhood (the cockney cat burglar had been singularly ill-inspired in his choice of terrain, the pickings would have been small, unattractive, rather vulgar, and not worth very much). Now Edward felt the need to distance himself physically from it. We took a tram to its terminus at the foot of a steep hill near the coast, then walked several miles along the hills high above Dublin Bay on its southern side. We went on for several hours, our appetites whetted by the wind off the sea. Eventually we stopped at a restaurant that overlooked the sea, and settled down to a most agreeable dinner. I think we even had a bottle of wine with it, for something must have contributed to the boisterousness of our spirits as we set off on the return journey. There was the added and still unfamiliar – I was only sixteen, Edward seventeen – excitement of being out late at night and of doing something normally forbidden; for we had been expected back for supper. We had missed the last tram from the terminus and had to walk the whole way back to Booterstown. It was well after midnight when we got back to No. 23; but the light was still on in Medea's bedroom, a warning light signalling wrath and row to come. Seeing it, Edward remarked, quite cheerfully, I think to keep up his

no doubt flagging morale: 'By now she'll be absolutely fuming.' He
went upstairs to verify her state, and very soon came down to report
that she put all the blame on me. *My* idea, of course, deliberately to
have missed supper and to have kept Edward out so late that she had
been unable to sleep for anxiety about him. Perhaps he had fallen
over the edge of a cliff, the cliff paths were so treacherous, especially
at night; and Edward was not familiar with them (in fact he had
explored them thoroughly for miles, knew their every turn).
Apparently, I had been expendable; it would not have mattered if I
had dropped thirty feet or so onto the jagged rocks below; but as I too
had, rather inconsiderately, returned, I was to be put on the boat that
very day. I was not to stay a day longer. She would telegraph my
parents first thing in the morning.

At least my sentence was delivered to me through an intermediary.
I was to go unseen and unheard; I did not have to face Medea. This
was a minor mercy; if she could no longer bear to set eyes on the
English evil influence, I was very relieved to be deprived of another
sight of her. In fact, I never saw her again, my last viewing of her had
been during the exchange of missiles in the drawing-room. Edward
sent off the telegram early in the morning, before accompanying me
to Dun Laoghaire. I was not at all upset by the sudden termination of
my Irish holiday ten days before it was due to have ended; I was even
happy to see the white letters of BOYCOTT BRITISH GOODS
receding in the wake of the mailboat. I had had quite enough of the
Free State; I had had more than enough of bad theatre, and quite
looked forward to the predictability of Tunbridge Wells and the
sanity of England.

When I got home my mother did not express any surprise at the
suddenness of my return. She even claimed that she had predicted
something of the sort, for she had realised from the start that my
friend's mother was totally unreliable and feckless; she had had the
greatest misgivings about my going there in the first place, but had

allowed herself to be overruled by my father, who, having spent most of his active life in various parts of Africa, starting in the Cape and ending up in the Soudan, had a firmly held belief in the educational effects of foreign travel as a condition of 'character-building'. A Dublin holiday, he had argued, would make a welcome change from Tankerton, Deal, St Margaret's Bay or Gorran Haven, our usual holiday spots. I was old enough now, it appeared, to go off somewhere on my own. She had let him have his way on this occasion in the knowledge that he was already seriously ill with suspected cancer of the throat. My mother had a habit of being proved in the right by the course of subsequent events; and she had always expressed a healthy distrust of the Irish, male or female. They were dirty, feckless and profligate. She did not blame me at all for what had happened, and made no reference to the telegram (save to observe that the sender did not know how to spell) nor to its contents (which, as dictated by Medea, would certainly have included utterly fantastic allegations – the Ruin of My Boy and that sort of thing – that would reflect her taste for cheap drama). My mother's last word on the subject was that my hostess was clearly an impossible woman.

In fact, I was more than compensated for the sudden curtailment of my first exposure to 'abroad'. I went off to spend the next ten days in Cambridge with the parents and sisters of my friend Jo Clover: quiet, kind, gentle people who never raised their voices and who *drank* their tea. Clover and I did the colleges, the Backs, the Castle Mound, the Botanical Gardens; we went to see my aunt in Girton, and had a delicious cream tea in a pretty village, the main street of which I sketched in pen-and-ink. The tea-shop was run by two well-spoken ladies in smocks. In the evenings, we sat reading while Clover's father dropped off over his chess-set, pulling himself out of sleep every now and then with a startled twitch. His mother and his aunt, Miss Clover, seemed to know an enormous number of dons; and the Clovers seemed to have been in Cambridge for generations.

Clover was perhaps a shade too earnest for my naturally flippant tastes, and he tended to take things rather too seriously. He worried about the state of the world, South Wales, unemployment, all of which seemed to me very remote from Tunbridge Wells. But he was very proud of Cambridge and took a delight in showing me its wealth of buildings and gardens. The waters of the Cam seemed to flow with reassuring sluggishness, and I had had quite enough of drama.

The summer holidays of 1934 ended as peacefully as usual under a wide and windy sky. I quite looked forward to the new term and the expectations of what it might bring: an attempt to get my school running colours, the Bright History Prize, sitting for an award at an Oxford college on a trial run, the joys of the history sixth, the town Art Club. I was pretty sick of Moloch, Medea and the lot of them.

7

Mr Simon

I really thought, in the autumn of 1934, that I was clear of Medea and her entourage, and that I could put the Dublin minor catastrophe safely behind me, as an unpleasant episode best forgotten about, even if my stay there had had its moments of high comedy. Indeed, even this is to put it too positively; as far as I was concerned, the Medea chapter was now closed. I was sick of that penny-coloured chronicle. Increasingly bored by the dreadfully repetitive mother and son act, I made the mistake of thinking that my own growing indifference to the latest episode in the never-ending Booterstown story would be reflected in Medea's corresponding indifference towards someone who had only been the briefest of guests. But I had not reckoned with the sheer tenacity of the woman's malevolence. Slothful, unimaginative, uneducated, ignorant, feckless, sloppily dishonest – she fell into dishonesty, fell out of it again if it involved too much effort – changeable, untruthful, untidy, she could give evidence of a quite uncharacteristic energy and single-mindedness in the pursuit of her personal vendettas, concentrating entirely on each one in succession. Indeed I should have realised that such concentration was a natural by-product of her sloth and intellectual indigence. Having nothing to occupy her mind, she could give herself entirely to the pursuit of vengeance. I suppose it was one way of getting her through the day.

It had not occurred to me that I would be the next one on her list; I had not thought myself that important. I had believed that my summary expulsion and, as she would have seen it through her usual enlarging lenses, disgrace, would have been enough to have satisfied her taste for cheap drama. She would surely soon be back to her old tricks, attempting to fiddle the Irish Sweep or be busying herself, in a half-hearted way, in some other vaguely shabby undertaking. But I had completely underestimated her viciousness. She had probably been immensely peeved by the knowledge, passed on by Edward, that my mother had dismissed her ravings for what they were: the hysteria of an histrionic Irishwoman. Foolishly, I had continued to write to Edward, after my aborted visit, in order to be kept *au fait* with Medea's doings and malpractices, tantrums and threats. Medea was, to some extent, our common property, perhaps the only subject that still kept us together. So I had maintained a minor flow of enquiries and allusions in my correspondence with him during the remainder of the holidays.

Quite early in the new term, my mother – my father was by then in the Radium Institute – received a letter from Miley & Miley, a firm of Dublin solicitors acting on behalf of their client, Edward's mother. I never actually saw the letter; but its gist was clear and very threatening. They had been instructed to prepare a libel suit against my parents, in view of the fact that, as a minor, I could not be sued. My mother first consulted her own solicitor, Mr Snell, a Salopian who, as such, enjoyed her complete confidence. He was not at all reassuring; he told her that the plaintiff had a very strong case and that, in the event of the suit going forward, heavy damages might be awarded. There must be some means of preventing the case from coming up. He even advised settling out of court. At the same time Edward, whom I consulted as soon as I had heard from my mother, told me that his mother was on the warpath, that she was determined to ruin me, as I had ruined her son; all the usual histrionics, in fact.

But it was more than her usual posturing. For Edward went on to tell me that, after he had returned to Shrewsbury, Medea had been through the wardrobe in his bedroom in St Helen's Road, clearing out the contents of the pockets of his suits and jackets. Knowing his mother's habits, he should have known better than to have left any letters or papers in his clothes. He had been extraordinarily careless. For she must have been quite delighted by what she had found: there were several letters addressed by me to Edward in the last weeks of the holidays. In one of them, referring to her, of course, as Medea – I could think of no other name for her by then – I had made several allusions to what was said to have happened at about the time of Edward's birth, or shortly after it. She had, so her son had told me several times, attempted to poison her husband, the doctor, by putting a massive dose of arsenic in a dish set aside for his supper. But the dish had at once gone off course – this I could well imagine, she would have been sure to have made a hash of the operation – and it had been eaten by the living-in maid, who had narrowly escaped death, but had been saved, *in extremis*, by the doctor, who had administered a stomach pump on the poor girl throughout the night. By the morning, she had been out of danger. No charges had been preferred, the police had not been informed, but Edward's father had ordered his wife out of the house forthwith.

All this was pretty strong stuff for a schoolboy from a middle-class family in Tunbridge Wells. I had been treated to the story several times over, and had never doubted its veracity. Edward was convinced it had been true. Of course, it was very foolish of me to have referred to it in writing, even in a private letter, though I could not have foreseen that a letter addressed to my friend would eventually fall into the clutches of his mother; and as it was a private letter, I thought that it could not be taken as a public libel. But I was no lawyer. Nor was this the full extent of the damage. In several other letters that she had deposited with her solicitors, I had jokingly asked whether she had yet carried out the Liffey operation; and, if not, when was she going to? What was she waiting for? Why did she not get on with it? The sooner the better. All this was accompanied by the usual schoolboy jokes about not taking the car with her in this ultimate, and long overdue, journey. Could she not be persuaded to leave the little car at the quayside? I think, too, there may have been a bit about sex. Edward and I had read a book by Robert Bruce-Lockhart in which there was a reference to the body of a St Petersburg prostitute which had been discovered in an apartment house by some Red Guards who, at the sight, had exclaimed, with disgust: *prostitutka*, or something of the kind, and this, for some reason, we had found highly suggestive, so that we peppered our letters with the code word *stutka*. It was perfectly harmless, more schoolboy stuff, but Miley & Miley picked on it as proof of the role I had been assigned as a moral corrupter of Irish innocence.

My mother informed Mr Hardy, the headmaster of Shrewsbury, of what was impending, and he was sufficiently alarmed to suggest that she come up from Kent to discuss what could be done to prevent the case from going forward. If the case did come up, he seemed to think I would have to leave the school. (My housemaster, Ferret-Face, was quite delighted by this unexpected piece of good fortune, telling my mother quite baldly that I would have to go and that this would endanger my prospects of going on to Oxford.) So my mother came up and remained closeted with Mr and Mrs Hardy in the drawing-room of Kingsland House, while I waited nervously outside in the hall to hear the verdict. When she came out, she seemed considerably reassured, not that she had ever displayed any outward sign of alarm. Mr Hardy had the stern appearance of a rather inflexible moralist who might have been thought to have been unsympathetic, even condemnatory, in a crisis of this kind. But his appearance was quite deceptive; he was in fact a very kind and understanding man, and he was not lacking in worldly wisdom. He made light of the *stutka* business, dismissing it for what it was: silly adolescent stuff. The references to the attempted murder he treated much more seriously. He had told my mother, at the beginning of the interview, that he had encountered this sort of situation on a previous occasion, in his position as headmaster of Cheltenham. It was, it seemed, not unusual for a public schoolboy to be sued for libel. He had a suggestion to make; it might not work, but it was certainly worth trying. Richard would have to go up to London at once and see a friend of his. There was only one course of action that could prevent the libel suit from going forward. It would be quite expensive: two fees of fifty guineas each; but he thought that would do the trick.

I was to go up to London on the following day – he had already arranged a consultation for me on the phone for the morning of the day after that – and I was to see a well-known Wimpole Street psychiatrist, Mr Simon, an old friend of his. Mr Simon would ask me a few questions which I would have to answer quite straightforwardly; there would be no catch. He would ask me if I had not been working rather intensively – overdoing it, perhaps – in preparation for sitting for an award at an Oxford College towards the end of the current term. Had I been sleeping properly? Had I been staying up at night, long after Lights Out? Had I not been subject to undue strain and anxiety? Had I not also been worrying about my father's health? He was sure that Mr Simon would understand the situation, in fact he had spelt it out in detail to him over the phone. He thought – he could not be sure, of course – that, after talking to me for half an hour or so, he would be able to draw up a medical attestation to the effect that, in the course of the previous two months – that would cover it, would it not? – I had, as a result of a combination of overwork and worry about my father's health, undergone a temporary mental breakdown, and that I could not be held legally responsible for anything that I had written during that period. This would not mean, of course that I was being certified, or even that there was any suggestion of insanity, nothing like that: just that I had not really known what I was writing. There would have to be a second opinion; but Mr Hardy had seen to that, too. Later, on the same morning, I would call on a colleague of Mr Simon's, in the same street and only a couple of doors down from his consulting-room, who would ask me similar questions. With the attestation signed by two qualified consultants, it only remained to send it off to the Dublin solicitors. The case would have to be quashed. Mr Hardy actually grinned while evoking the prospect, adding, in a confidential tone, that, in all his experience, both as a housemaster, then as a headmaster of two public schools, he had never had to deal with a parent as trouble-some, as difficult and as unreliable as Edward's mother: 'a truly appalling woman', he concluded, with warmth. My mother fully concurred with this judgment. The headmaster and she understood one another perfectly. Mrs Hardy then confirmed that there had been a similar case with a boy at Cheltenham and that all had been settled satisfactorily, in the manner the headmaster had outlined. When the three came out into the vestibule, they were all smiling. Mrs Hardy, a good-looking lady with a very gentle face, came up to me, saying: 'It will be all right, Richard, you will see'.

All this trouble was happening to my poor mother just at the time when she had learnt that there was little hope for my father, despite the treatment at the Radium Institute. But she seemed to be taking it all in her stride and she was very grateful to Mr and Mrs Hardy for their kindness and their encouragement. As a doctor's daughter, she also knew what a Wimpole Street address could do. During her short stay in Shrewsbury, she had telephoned one of her brothers, who had a medical practice in Cheyne Walk; and he could not speak too warmly of Mr Simon, a man at the very top of his profession, with many initials after his name (and, for my mother, medical initials spoke with more authority even than a Dukedom). There was no doubt, she added, that we were going to the right man. She also said that for the two nights I would be spending in London, I would be staying with my uncle, a great favourite of mine, and my Greek aunt, a royalist and keen partisan of the exiled King George of the Hellenes (his signed photograph, in a silver frame, stood on a table in her drawing-room; there was another of King Constantine). All this had already been arranged. While very sorry for having brought so much trouble and expense to my parents just at a time when my mother was having to cope on her own, I was of course delighted at the prospect of a mid-term break in London, especially in winter-time, when everything was on. My uncle and aunt treated me like an adult, they knew a great many interesting people, both English and Greek; and I would be free to do anything I liked in the evening. I could be a real man about town at the very moment when the boys in my house would be settling down to evening prep.

On my first night in London I went to see a film at the New Gallery. Before the film – which I cannot remember – there was an absolutely amazing newsreel of the assassination of King Alexander of Jugoslavia and of Monsieur Louis Barthou, the French Foreign Minister, on the Canebière, in Marseilles. There was even a shot of the king, through the open rear door of the car – I think it was a Panhard-Levassor – lying on the floor; one could see his rimless glasses that had fallen off a few inches from his head. People in uniform wearing white gloves and peaked caps were shouting, blowing whistles and waving their arms, running up and down. There was an officer in a helmet and wearing a dark uniform on a rearing horse; to the right of the car, which had stopped, the chauffeur had got out. The horseman kept on raising his long, crescent-shaped sabre, and bringing it down hard on the back of a man in civilian clothes: down it came, again and again, as the man bent lower and lower, sinking to his knees, then lying on the ground. He had been holding a revolver, but under the hail of blows, he dropped it; one could see it shining on the wet *pavé* between the silver tramlines. The newsreel went on for several minutes. The cameramen seemed to have been the only people present at the scene who knew what they were doing. Everyone else appeared to be running this way and that, their mouths open; some of them had what looked like white or red lanyards at their shoulders. It was fascinating and very frightening. I had never seen anything like it: assassination in motion, move by move. I believe the newsreel was not shown in France, at least at the time. The car had only got a few yards from the landing-stage at the Vieux-Port. There is a big white monument at the level of where it happened. The newsreel at least helped me to get the purpose of my unexpected presence in London in proportion. It made Medea and her malevolence seem oddly irrelevant and a bit provincial. I thought after that that I could face up to Mr Simon. He would understand.

The next day I was at least half an hour early for my appointment with him. I had been admitted by a very smart maid, who had taken me into a beautifully furnished waiting-room. I picked up the *Illustrated London News*; the assassination of King Alexander was not in it. I suppose it had only happened a day or two before. But there was a whole page of photographs of Bruno Hauptmann in hand-cuffs between two tall men in light-coloured stetsons. He was awaiting trial for the murder of the Lindbergh baby. I was still reading about him and looking at photographs of the Lindbergh country house from which the baby had been snatched, when the maid came in and said that Mr Simon was ready to see me, taking me across the passage and opening the door to a big room that faced onto a small, very trim garden, with a fountain, a sundial and the statue of a faun. Mr Simon was a very small man, owl-like behind very large horn-rimmed glasses. He had very bright eyes, and these he never took off my face throughout the interview which lasted – I discovered when I came out and looked at a grandfather clock in the hall – nearly fifty minutes. Although his eyes never left my face, he kept on making notes on a pad. He was very friendly and gentle; he spoke in a low voice and had some sort of foreign accent. I at once felt completely at ease with him, answering all his questions without difficulty; my answers just came out. I had been rehearsing what I would say, but it was not like that all. He seemed pleased enough with my answers, as if they had been what he had expected, commenting every now and then: 'So', 'so', 'Yes, I see.' At the end, he got up, thanked me for having been so helpful, and shook my hand. I had never been treated with such elaborate politeness. My visit to his colleague two doors down was very brief: only a quarter of an hour. He seemed to know all the answers in advance, and kept on looking at a sheet of notes on the table in front of him. At the end he said: 'That will be all, then, thank you very much', and also shook my hand. I cannot remember anything about his appearance, save that he had a morning coat and haircord trousers. I think he had a pince-nez. We were still in the pince-nez decades: the Pope had one, all American senators seemed to have them, my first dentist in Tunbridge Wells wore one. He too had a funny accent, but it was not the same as Mr Simon's.

I came away from the two interviews, as one might come away from a written examination: I might have done very well, or I might have completely muffed it, got everything wrong. But when I got back to Cheyne Walk and saw my uncle's face and his laughing eyes, I realised that I had done all right. He had been on the phone to both of his colleagues. Apparently they had been delighted with my responses to their questioning. It was an absolutely clear case of overwork resulting in temporary mental breakdown. There was nothing to fear for the future; I was already on the road to full recovery. The document had been signed and counter-signed; it would be delivered to his surgery that very afternoon, and he would be sending it straight on to my mother. He had already talked to her and to Mr Hardy on the phone to tell them that everything had gone according to plan and that the two consultants had been most impressed by my answers. I felt a bit of a fraud: I had not been the least bit ill; I had contented myself with answering, as directly as possible, the questions that had been put to me, and I had greatly enjoyed this mid-term interlude in the wonderful and entirely unexpected freedom of a brightly lit-up wintry London. I felt that I must have achieved something; everyone seemed so pleased with me – my Greek aunt was positively effusive, even giving me rather a sploshy kiss – though I was not sure just what I had achieved. But I rejoiced in the knowledge that Medea had been stopped in her tracks. How she would fume, when Miley & Miley told her of the document! And, indeed, I learnt from a joyful Edward, a week or so later, that she had been absolutely beside herself with impotent rage, taking it out on what was left of the china. He had had a letter from his mother's daily about the damage; the woman had written to him because she was worried about her mistress's mental state. Apparently she had been talking to herself, ranting and raving, between the smashing sessions, and had then taken to her bed for the best part of a week. The house had been even filthier than usual, and the daily had not been allowed to tidy the place up. On the other hand, the operation had cost my parents a hundred guineas, a lot of money in those days; and it has since occurred to me that Mr Snell and the headmaster may have over-reacted to the threat of a libel action that had originated in the misuse of a private letter addressed to a third party. But I suppose they were right not to have taken any chances.

Once again I thought that this would be the last I would hear of Medea. But she was not the sort of person to give up even after such a major setback. I did not know about her next move at the time, only hearing of it much later, in February 1936. Apparently, once she had risen from her disordered bed of rage, she had set out, in her green ink, childish, sloping hand-writing, and erratic spelling, to write to the head of each of the Oxford male colleges to inform him of the interesting fact that, among those who would be sitting for college awards in the entrance exams to be held in the following month, December 1934, there was a boy from Shrewsbury called

Richard Cobb who had *ruined her son*, who was a thief and a burglar, a cheat and a liar, corrupt and utterly immoral, and quite unsuited to be admitted to any decent, self-respecting institution. She had been unable to find out from Edward – who would not have known in any case – not only which group of colleges I would be sitting for, but even which of the two ancient universities (for she had known of the connection of my mother's family with Cambridge). So she had written to the head of each Cambridge male college as well. She must have written something like fifty letters in all, warning Provosts, Presidents, Rectors, Masters, Wardens, Deans (I expect she got them all hopelessly wrong) of the evil influence about to beat at their doors for admission; but there was still time to prevent the irreparable. Let them heed the Cry of a Mother and be forewarned, or other young men, many other young men, would, like her son, be ruined. It was only in the course of another crisis, in the middle of my second term at Merton, that I first heard of the existence of this extraordinary correspondence. 'Oh yes,' said Mr Harrison, the Principal of the Postmasters (Scholars), 'I do vaguely remember now, the Warden had a most intemperate letter from a mad Irishwoman denouncing you for all manner of crimes, I think it may have helped you get your Postmastership: we thought, this man Cobb, from Shrewsbury, he must be rather an unusual person to have provoked such a wild outburst.' He said that the letter had somehow fixed my name in the awareness of the fellows most concerned with College Entrance; furthermore, as my interview had been conducted by two historians from University College, they had said that the Master of that college had been in receipt of a similar missive. Unfortunately, he was unable to show me a copy of Medea's literary masterpiece: the old Warden had burnt it in his grate, after showing it to some of the fellows, saying that the fire was the right place for that sort of thing. Mr Harrison's revelation was a reminder that Medea's innate stupidity ran neck and neck with her vigorous malevolence. It would certainly never have occurred to her that a letter so intemperate, so ill-written and so histrionic could actually have indirectly benefited the object of its lurid contents. I like to think that, even now, in some college archive, whether in Oxford or in Cambridge, there still exists one of her green-written diatribes. Such evidence of ill-composed, inflated malevolence deserves to be preserved, if only as a small monument to the memory of a woman who was as nasty as she was unintelligent. It would certainly be more expressive of what she was really like than anything I could do for her.

So I did not know at the time that Edward's mother, dipping her pen into her bottle of green ink and writing the same letter, was so diligently and silently working on my behalf. I wish I had known; I would have felt flattered and encouraged to have been the subject of such uncharacteristic energy and industry. I hardly gave Medea a thought after the quashing of the libel suit. Having obtained the Postmastership in history at Merton in December 1934, I was asked, politely but firmly, to leave Shrewsbury at once. I think I may have owed this abrupt, quite unexpected, but, as far as I was concerned, welcome decision to the combined malevolence of Medea and Ferret-Face, an unusual, but, after all, suitable alliance between near-equals in awfulness. At least I like to think that it may have been so; for, in that case, Edward's mother might be said not only to have contributed, in some small way, to my gaining an award at Merton, but that also she may have been indirectly responsible for my switch from the study of the vast correspondence of the great Duke of Newcastle – I obtained a reader's ticket to the Manuscript Room of the British Museum at seventeen and a bit – to that of the French Revolution, as a result of the decision taken by my mother to send me off to Paris. Anyhow, I spent much of 1935 in Paris and in Strasbourg, while Edward stayed on at Shrewsbury for the rest of the school year. I only saw him once in the course of that year, during a brief visit to London in March – we stayed together a couple of nights in someone's flat in Kensington, displaying ourselves once more in spats and boaters. I seem to remember too that we rang up Madame Roussel at her Dublin home, claiming to be a London theatrical agency and offering to put on one of her edifying plays about the triumph of innocence over vice. But it was only an interlude, a very brief relapse into juvenilia. I had to go on to Tunbridge Wells to see my poor father, now terribly emaciated and with his clothes hanging loosely from him. He was in the last stages of cancer of the throat. I had quite got out of the dangerous habit of writing to my friend. But he may have gone on writing to me; I feel pretty sure that he did, for he was always very anxious not to lose his longest-standing audience of one (though I discovered about this time that I had had a successor, or several successors in this essential role). In his letters, he gave me regular reports of Medea's misdeeds, woes and tantrums and of Moloch's scheming designs, in a rather appealing effort to keep me abreast of the old chronicle of family warfare. He seemed to live in and for his family *roman fleuve*. But I had moved on, and once I had gone up to Oxford, meeting new friends and acquiring new interests, the old familiar nicknames of adolescence, Moloch, Medea, and the rest of them, had all seemed to have become increasingly remote and irrelevant.

8

February, 1936

It was a clear blustery day, the pavements still wet from the sharp showers at the end of the night. It was still quite early in the fresh morning and I had just reached the level of Queen's on my way back from a visit to my tutor, who lived off the cloisters in Magdalen, to get the subject of my next essay, when I met Brian Inglis, who had been on the History Side with me at Shrewsbury, and who was now an undergraduate at Magdalen, coming the other way. I remember thinking how good-looking he was with his bright colouring and abundant curly hair. He looked excited and was smiling broadly, as if he were particularly pleased to see me at that moment. When he had come level with me, he asked me if I had seen *The Times* of that morning – I think it was a Tuesday – and I said that I had not yet seen any of the papers. He told me that there was a short news item under some such heading as WIFE OF FAMOUS DUBLIN SURGEON MISSING, and that Edward's mother had disappeared. He went on to say that they were looking for her off the coast. 'I reckon Edward must have done it' – Brian's home was in Swords, to the north side of Dublin Bay, and he was as well-informed of the doings of Edward's family as I was – 'don't you?' I agreed that it seemed likely. And we both burst out laughing, I don't quite know why. I suppose because it was so very predictable, so much what we would both have expected of Edward. We'd both been so often served with such portentous statements as: 'You'll see, there'll be a drama in my family one of these days.' We laughed in the appreciation of a shared joke, and as if we had both seen it coming all the time, from very far back (Brian had been at prep school with Edward, even farther back than myself). I suppose we felt that our mutual friend had at last fulfilled himself, in the only way he could have, as much as to say, triumphantly: 'You did not believe me, did you? You did not think me capable of it? Admit it'. I don't think either of us gave a thought to Edward's mother, to what might have happened to her, save that it was certainly something pretty nasty; it was the old Edward up to his tricks again, and this time it really looked as if he had stepped well beyond the limits of schoolboy tomfoolery, even if it were only an extension of the old familiar call for attention. I was glad to have had the news from Brian, the one person then in Oxford who, like myself, could see the thing from inside. Neither of us had the slightest doubt that, whatever had happened, it had been Edward's doing.

All the papers carried reports about the missing woman, who did not seem to exist in her own right, but only as the wife of a famous man (from whom she had been separated for nearly ten years). It seemed rather unfair on Medea, who had an awfulness quite of her own. The popular dailies gave more details than the bald item in *The Times*. One, the *Mirror*, I think, even had people on the look-out on the Welsh coast. I did not feel like laughing after that. I went up to my room and promptly burnt all the letters that I had received from Edward over the previous eighteen months. There was little hope that he would have done the same with mine; luckily, I had sent him very harmless items about my activities in France. I had never even referred to his mother since our last meeting nearly a year before. Having destroyed his letters and raked up the ashes, there did not seem much more that I could do for the moment. There was not much point in leaving my comfortable scholarly retreat and in going out as it were to meet the trouble halfway; the trouble would be bound to seek me out sooner or later. I went on working as before, attending tutorials, writing my two weekly essays, working in the Bodleian, running round the Meadows first thing in the morning or using the Iffley Road track in the afternoon, going out with two or

three of my friends to a pub in the evening to play shove-ha'penny.
Such a rigorous attachment to the daily and weekly routine seemed
to offer a barrier against anything unpleasant that might come from
outside, and more especially from the other shore of the Irish
Channel. I could see no reason for telling the college authorities
what might happen, before it actually happened; they might not have
believed me in any case, for this looked like something quite out of
line with the usual problems of college discipline.

Meanwhile, there were more and more details coming out in the
papers. As if to confirm our rather tasteless fantasies about leaving
the car at the quayside of the Liffey, the Baby Austin appeared
indeed to have survived its owner; it had soon been discovered a few
feet above the shore at Shankill, ten miles south of Dublin (where
Edward and I had walked on the last night of my stay in Booterstown). There were traces of human skin and bits of hair and
bloodstains on the back seat, as well as on a large plaid rug. But there
was still no sign of the body. Then, while under close observation by
the police and just before being formally charged with the murder of
his mother, it was reported that Edward had asked permission to go
up to the lavatory and had thrown himself through the bathroom
window, breaking a vertebra in his neck so that he was sent first of all
to the infirmary of the Mountjoy, before being put in a cell. Soon
after that, much to my astonishment – and alarm – I started getting
letters from him, from his cell in the Mountjoy. In the first letter
there was also a rather illiterate scrawl written by one of the warders,
introducing himself to me as Michael Feeney. He said he would be
smuggling out Edward's letters to me regularly, putting them in
ordinary envelopes and posting them through the normal mail, for as
long as my friend stayed there while awaiting trial before the Dublin
High Court. Feeney wrote that he had wanted to do something for
the poor boy, he was so charming. Here was yet another example of
my friend's amazing ability to get round people.

Edward's letters were quite jaunty in tone, as if he were actually enjoying a rather unusual experience. He told me that he was reading all the papers, English and Irish, and he seemed quite gratified by all the publicity surrounding his case. (Feeney told me, when I met him in Dublin in the summer of 1938, that Edward had made himself extremely unpopular with the other prisoners, thanks to the avidity with which he devoured all the papers. They had felt that there was something indecent about his need to read about what he had done; after all, he had been accused of killing his mother, and for most of the inmates there could have been nothing worse than that; and, at one stage he had had to be put in a cell on his own in order to prevent him from being physically assaulted). I remember that his principal concern in these letters to me was to convince me that the whole thing had been premeditated and very carefully planned; he kept on coming back to that. I burnt all the letters sent through Feeney as soon as I had read them. I was convinced that, sooner or later, my rooms in college would be searched. Perhaps it was I now who was beginning to overdramatise the situation in which I had found myself. If not dramatic, it was certainly a bizarre one.

I heard, first from my mother, that the English CID, acting on behalf of their Dublin counterparts, had been to my home in Tunbridge Wells. They did not have a warrant, had not searched my bedroom, and had been polite and rather apologetic; they had told her that they had hoped to find me, as they had wanted to ask me a certain number of questions. They had seemed surprised not to have found me at home; she had told them that I was an undergraduate at Oxford and that it was now the university term. Then came an agitated letter from Mr Hardy; three detectives had turned up on Kingsland in order to interview me. Fortunately they had not been at all conspicuous and had acted with discretion. He had received them in his study, and he had told them that I had left the school well over a year before, and that I was now studying at Oxford; he even gave them the name of my college. I could not understand why they were taking so long in tracking me down if they really wanted to question me; they seemed awfully dilatory, or awfully inefficient, or perhaps there was some more sinister reason for what looked like delaying tactics; they might be trying to frighten me into taking some foolish action, such as going abroad. Equally, they might think me too unimportant to be worth the effort of a third journey. But then why had they taken the other two? It could only be a matter of time before the three of them turned up. But still no one did, and it was now three weeks since the morning Brian had told me the news.

Meanwhile, Mr Hardy arranged to meet me over tea at the Great Western Hotel in Paddington. He said it was a matter of the gravest importance and could not wait. I agreed to meet him there on the following day. I arrived in good time in the enormous cretonned drawing-room. The place seemed to be filled by country clergymen and their wives, not unsuitable company, I thought, for my old headmaster. I at once spotted him ensconced in a deep armchair and reading a magazine, a familiar figure in a, to me, surprising pose. I had always seen him standing – he was a tall man, all public school headmasters have to be, there must be some sort of minimum requirement. Now, as if to emphasise that he was off-duty, he was actually reclining among the cushions of the chair. He looked very relieved, greeted me most cordially, and asked me to take the chair next to his. We had an excellent tea. He told me, in a low voice, and with great satisfaction, that he had had a very busy day, but that it had been worth the trouble; he had done the rounds of Fleet Street and its neighbourhood, he had been to see the editors of all the leading national dailies and weeklies, and he had managed to persuade them that there should be no mention of the school in their reports about the case: just that Edward had been 'educated at a well-known English public school', no more. Well, there could be no harm in that, it might be anywhere. He had, he said – and he was much given to such vigorous metaphors – managed to plug the breach in the dam, or almost, for he still had to go up to Manchester to see the people at the *Manchester Guardian*; he did not think there would be any trouble with them, and he would do the *Liverpool Daily Post* on the same day, using his Unitarian contacts. They were very influential up there, he told me, as if it were a matter of common knowledge. This was very important, he added, lowering his voice and taking a side look at the assembled clergy and their sensibly-clothed wives as they worked their way steadily through buttered toast, crumpets and seed cake, as if it would be improper for him to be heard referring respectfully to people who were presumably heretics, or at least not quite proper Christians. The school, he went on, had many connections with that part of the world.

He certainly emerged from this high-level interview as a man with many unexpected gifts. There had been his prompt recommendation of Mr Simon to my mother, and now here he was successfully inducing the papers to keep the name of Shrewsbury School out of all their reports. There was a good deal more guile than one would have credited him with if one were to go on his external appearance and rather military bearing. Mr Hardy seemed to know his way round the most unlikely places. Anyhow, he must have managed to square the *Guardian* and the *Daily Post*, as well as the London papers, for neither made any mention of the school. From the moment of my friend's arrest till the end of his trial, which was to be given very full coverage in all the English press, the school was never mentioned by name, at least in the English papers (for I think his writ had not extended to the *Irish Independent*, though – predictably no doubt – the *Irish Times* was to do the right thing. Too many readers of that respectable paper in those days would have had sons across the water in term-time, at a school which was on the direct line from Holyhead. More surprisingly even the hard-hitting and the very amusing *Dublin Opinion* maintained a quite uncharacteristic discreet silence on the subject of Edward's education).

But Mr Hardy, having told me his good news and expecting me to share in it, was much less optimistic about my *own* immediate prospects. He thought it was certain that I would have to attend the trial as a prosecution witness and that, once in the box, I would be subjected to a relentless pounding from Edward's counsel. Mud would be thrown at me in large quantities, adding, not unkindly, as he buttered a fourth scone, that mud that was thrown was liable to stick. Perhaps he had convoked me to Paddington to tell me that. He expressed sympathy at my predicament, but of course I had long ceased to be his prime concern. He had no concrete suggestions to offer me. I wondered rather why he had thought it so important that we should meet as a matter of such urgency when all that he had to offer me – apart from an extremely good tea and the reassuring presence of the West Country clergy – were one or two platitudes, a series of victory bulletins concerning the school, and the prospect of a pretty unpleasant time ahead as far as I was concerned. Perhaps he had not foreseen the full extent of his success in squaring the press. At least he had wanted to talk to me about the new situation brought about by Edward's arrest. I left him, feeling grateful, but a bit lonely. It looked as if I could not count on much help from outside.

But I was entirely wrong. It must have been almost a month after the disappearance of Edward's mother that the police at last came round to Merton, as if they had had difficulty in discovering the place and had only just stumbled upon it. I had expected three callers, as there had been three at my mother's and another three – or the same trio – at the school; but this time there was only *one*, as if, in the course of the previous weeks, my importance to the matter in hand had been diminished by two-thirds. That was one way of looking at it. On the other hand, the caller was pretty important. He was Chief Inspector Fox, of the Oxford CID. At some later date, he was to become Chief Constable of Oxfordshire. He turned up at the lodge one day, at a time when I was in college. He did not have a warrant, but he told the porter, Mr Innes, that he would like to see me in order to ask me a few questions. His request was referred to Mr Harrison, who then went to the law tutor, Mr Lawson. The latter, already a brilliant comparative lawyer, as well as a marvellous tutor, I think rather welcomed a situation that involved all sorts of complicated legal points and erudite matters of university privilege concerning resident members. Mr Lawson sent for me and told me that I was not to leave the college while the matter was being sorted out in discussions between himself and the Chief Inspector. As long as I was in college I had nothing to fear, as I was on privileged terrain. I was not even to go out into Merton Street, where I would be in danger, as subject to ordinary laws. So I was confined to Merton for the next five days while negotiations proceeded between the parties concerned. While I was not allowed out of college, Mr Fox was not allowed into it, beyond the lodge. Even the front quad was barred to him. I appreciated the importance of what had all the appearances of a frontier dispute. Eventually a compromise agreement was come to. The Chief Inspector was to be allowed into college and would be given the opportunity of putting his questions to me in Mr Lawson's rooms and in his presence. The law tutor would advise me as to whether I should answer any particular question or should refuse to answer it. It was quite apparent that Mr Lawson, quite apart from his own concern for my interests – he was a very kind and generous man who would do anything for his pupils – was greatly enjoying the whole business, for it seemed to raise all sorts of abstruse points of legal interpretation; and he was a very doughty fighter against bureaucracy.

So I went to Mr Lawson's room at the appointed time. It was at once clear to me that I had nothing to fear. Mr Fox was apologetic, very kind and gentle, and very nice. He started off by saying that he thought the Dublin CID were making mountains out of a very little molehill, and that, in his view, my involvement in the case seemed to be at most peripheral. Still, he had been instructed to ask me certain specific questions and to clear up two or three points, and this he would do, if, turning to Mr Lawson, that was all right; my tutor nodded that it was. Well, first of all, there was the question of my alibi. He did not think there would be any difficulty about that, as the murder had taken place in term-time. But the Dublin police were apparently going on the assumption that Edward must have had an accomplice; the missing woman weighed over fourteen stone – no wonder there had been so much power behind the forward thrust of the flying teapot – and it seemed unlikely to them that her son, thickset though he was, could have carried her body into the sea on his own. As my letters had been discovered among the papers relating to the abortive libel action, I was an obvious candidate for that role. There was no difficulty at all about establishing a cast-iron alibi. On the day of the murder I had been to chapel, had signed on for breakfast, lunch and Hall in the evening, had signed the tea book, had attended one of Mr Lawson's mammoth tutorials from nine to one, and had read my history tutor an essay at five in the afternoon – not so much a double piece of good fortune, but an outstanding example of virtue rewarded, and one that I have often quoted to my own pupils, for their benefit and mine: 'Never miss a tutorial'. Suppose I had missed both of mine that day. Where would I have been for the proving of my alibi? So that disposed of that. I could not have been in Dublin on the day of the murder.

Mr Fox seemed actually relieved to have so quickly disposed of the accomplice theory, adding, perhaps a trifle unkindly, as he took in my skinny frame, that I did not look as if I would have been of much assistance in carrying a fourteen-stone body. He thought that they should have been looking for someone of rather different frame, and much nearer home. He then turned to his notes. The Dublin police had obviously not been over-sanguine on the subject of my alibi; so they had reserved for themselves a second line of attack as far as I was concerned: they were trying to establish a case of incitement to murder against me, on the basis of the letters that his mother had discovered in Edward's pockets. Had I not asked, several times, about his mother's often proclaimed intention of committing suicide? Had this not been an encouragement to Edward perhaps to do it for her? Had I not put him in mind of the possibility – and the material advantages – of her sudden death? But it at once transpired that no letters of mine had been found that had been written over the last two years, or none at least that contained phrases that might be construed as incitement (thank goodness, I thought, that I had taken such care not to repeat the rather silly jokes about the imminence of Operation Liffey!). Mr Lawson then made the point that incitement to murder, to be legally provable, had to be within a period of less than two years. Over a longer period, so it appeared from what he said, incitement would simply lose its sting, like coffee that had lost its flavour for having been kept too long. I was mighty pleased to hear about this. So that line too would have to be abandoned. Mr Fox again seemed genuinely pleased, commenting, with a smile, that the provocative remarks that I had made in my letters about leaving the car first at the quayside before she took the plunge and so on were 'just typical kids' stuff', schoolboy nonsense, to be dismissed as such. That was all, he said, folding up his papers. He would report back to the English CID, for forwarding to Dublin, that the result of the interview had been entirely negative, that I was completely in the clear, and that there would be no follow-up. He was about to leave, after shaking our hands most warmly, when, at Mr Lawson's door, he turned back, as if something had just occurred to him and that had not been in his brief. He asked me where I intended passing the Easter vacation. I was surprised at this question, because I could not see its relevance to what we had been discussing. So I said I would be going to Paris, as I usually did once term had ended. He advised me strongly not to do that. I could not understand why a police officer should have assumed the functions of a travel agency, so I was even more puzzled when he added: 'Go to Brussels'. I asked why I should go to Brussels rather than to Paris. He then explained that there was no extradition treaty between Belgium and the Irish Free State. The Chief Inspector went on to say that the prosecution were certain to try to *subpoena* me as a witness – but if I were to be in Belgium just before the trial opened and throughout its course – and from his instructions, it seemed likely that the trial would come up over Easter – they would be unable to do so. This was a very valuable piece of information, and one that had naturally not occurred to Mr Hardy, so wise in other ways. Mr Fox was obviously personally concerned for my welfare; and I was greatly moved by his kindness. For several years afterwards we sent each other Christmas cards; and I remember writing to congratulate him on his promotion to Chief Constable. There was another point in his favour: he did not seem to like the Irish very much. He said that he was quite certain that the Dublin CID had it in for me because I was English; and I am quite sure he was right.

So that was the end of that. Mr Lawson had visibly enjoyed the whole episode. My standing with my fellow undergraduates was much enhanced by the knowledge, rapidly spread, that I had been questioned in a murder case and had had to prove my alibi. As soon as term ended, I went off to Brussels, working in the Bibliothèque Royale, a charming eighteenth century Habsburg palace. Once the trial had begun, I bought the continental edition of the *Daily Mail* every day so as to follow it in detail. I have seldom enjoyed Brussels so much, and I had that comforting feeling of security that must have been experienced by so many French criminals and by so many political exiles from authoritarian regimes who had taken refuge there, in the knowledge that they were beyond the reach of repressive authorities or an inquiring police. I particularly savoured the frequent references to an English evil influence. And it was nice to hear from my mother that an unpleasant-looking legal document had arrived for me in Tunbridge Wells and that she had returned it to sender with the information that I was out of the country and would not be returning before the end of April or early-May. I think she even had the rather happy inspiration of giving them my Brussels address, *Hôtel de la Grande Cloche*, down in the Lower Town, where Verlaine and Rimbaud had once stayed and near where the elder man had taken a pot shot at the young poet, before being arrested. Yes, it had been the *subpoena* all right; Chief Inspector Fox had not underestimated the malevolence of the Dublin CID and of the prosecution counsel. As I read the reports of the trial, I realised what I had escaped. I seem to remember that an unfortunate temporary master at Shrewsbury who had struck up a friendship with Edward in the latter's last year at the school had had a *subpoena* served on him, had been obliged to attend the whole trial, and had been severely mauled by Edward's counsel. He had been assigned the place that had no doubt been for me. All in all, it was a very satisfying vacation. I used to treat myself to my daily exposure to the trial over an enormous and quite delicious *café-filtre* – the fact that I was where I was, and not but for the foresight of my friend, the Chief Inspector, where I might have been, made it taste all the *more* delicious – on the terrace of a café in the neighbourhood of the Place Brouckère. It was usually sunny, with a light wind and fast-moving fleecy clouds, and I divided my lingering breakfast between taking in the latest news of the trial, and watching the passers-by on the wide pavement, many of the rather pretty girls already in spring dresses.

I realised then, for the first time, that 'being abroad' has both a negative and a positive attraction, the negative one often being the stronger: that, for instance, of not being in England at a time when things there were particularly unpleasant and uncomfortable (there was a real pleasure to be derived from dwelling on the imagined details of such horrors from a decent distance), or, in this instance, of not being in Dublin, a feeling even more potent than the pull of unfamilarity and the excitement of moderate exoticism (Brussels was comfortably and reassuringly bourgeois, even a bit dowdy, there was nothing Mediterranean or violent about the place). It was a pleasure I was often to savour in later years.

There was no doubt that, from a distance, I had much enjoyed reading about Edward's trial. I was glad, too, that, despite his own disastrous appearances in the witness-box, where, to the consternation of his counsel, he had persisted in maintaining that he had premeditated his mother's murder and had carefully planned every stage of it – a fantasy that he continued doggedly to put out in all his correspondence with me, on lined notepaper headed with an embossed harp, over the next thirteen years – he had escaped the death penalty. He was declared guilty, but of unsound mind, and was condemned to be detained for such time 'as might be according to the Governor-General's pleasure', or some such formula. If he had been tried in England, I think he might well have been hanged; but Dublin in the thirties was a tight little provincial community, Edward's family were well-known, and the High Court judge had shown great sympathy for the young man's predicament. The year after his conviction, the Free State became Eire, the office of Governor-General being replaced by that of the President of the Republic, in the person of Dr Douglas Hyde. Edward found himself quite unwittingly at the centre of an important constitutional issue. His counsel appealed to the Irish Supreme Court – I think there was such a body – for the immediate release of his client, who, so he claimed, was being detained illegally. The grounds that he invoked in support of the appeal were that Edward's condemnation had been an exercise of the royal prerogative, and, the link with the Crown having been broken as the result of the formation of Eire and the election of its first President, it followed automatically that the sentence was invalid, and that in consequence he should either be set free, or should be re-tried. It was the sort of issue that would have greatly appealed to my tutor, Mr Lawson, the joint author, with my future Master, Sir David Lindsay Keir, of *Cases in Constitutional Law*. The judgment that resulted from the appeal proclaimed that the royal powers and privileges had automatically devolved on the person of the President of the Republic. I rather think that there had to be a formal re-trial, following which Edward was duly condemned to be detained for such time 'as might be according to the pleasure of the President of the Republic'; but I am not sure about either the re-trial or about the exact wording of the new formula. I do believe, however, that when, twelve years after this, Edward was finally released, the presidential powers were at least formally invoked, even though the decision had in fact been an administrative one, and had come either from the Minister of Justice or from the Minister of Home Affairs. In any case Edward left Ireland almost immediately and settled in London. He must have welcomed the opportunity to escape from the narrow provincialism of Dublin and to hide himself in the vast anonymity of London. However, he did return to Ireland for short visits to his half-sister much later on. I was quite surprised to hear of this when he told me very recently.

9

Footnotes

It is not my purpose to go over the horrifying circumstances of the actual murder at No. 23, nor to recount the details of the trial, as both have been very fully reported, both soberly and sensationally, in the English and Irish press, as well as in a book, *Memorable Irish Trials*.* I want only to add a few items that were not included in the newspaper reports, but that came to my knowledge either from what Edward told me at the time of our first meeting in Paris, or what he had written to me during his incarceration in Dundrum Asylum, or from what I had learnt from Cyril Monson, his former flat-mate, and from Michael Feeney, when I met them in the summer of 1938 in the course of my own personal investigation for the purpose of filling in some of the missing pieces.

Let us begin with his family – or what was left of it. Quite soon after the conclusion of the trial, his father remarried; his new wife, who had acted for many years as his surgery nurse, had, according to Edward, been his father's mistress for most of them. This may or may not have been so; it sounded like one of Medea's inventions. They started a new family; in fact, as I recently learnt, there was only one child, a daughter, Edward's half-sister, with whom he was later to establish friendly links. I know the doctor lived on to a ripe old age and that he drew much happiness from his new domestic situation. His practice – one of the best in Dublin – had certainly not suffered from the publicity brought by his son's trial. I cannot remember if he had been called as a witness; but I do know that he had induced

* By Kenneth E. L. Deale, Constable, London, 1960.

Edward's counsel to call, as witnesses for the defence, two well-known consultants, both psychiatrists. They had both given it as their opinion that the young man had been suffering from a severe mental condition, and the weight of their authority may have helped tip the balance in Edward's favour. Before these events, his father had had the double financial burden of assuring his separated wife's maintenance allowance and of paying for Edward's expensive education. Now, of course, he was relieved of both. For the next thirteen years, his son would be maintained in his basic needs by the Republic, while also enjoying a small private income inherited from his mother. I don't know whether his father ever visited him in Dundrum. But the eccentric and generous Madame Roussel visited him regularly, bringing him expensive fruit and groceries, as well as a steady supply of works of piety. She also prayed for him. There must have been some sort of reconciliation between father and son, for they seem to have met two or three times in later years, both in England and in Dublin. Again I only learnt of these meetings, at one of which at least Edward's elder brother John had been present, very recently.

But, outside the family, Edward had attracted attention in high places, and throughout all his time in the asylum he was visited regularly by Miss Dorothy McArdle, Eamon de Valera's secretary and biographer. Thanks to her intervention with the authorities, Edward was soon treated as a privileged prisoner; he was removed from a communal dormitory and was given a large room to himself with the double view that I have described. I think he was allowed to bring in some of his own furniture. He was also able to order any number of books and records. Throughout his stay in the asylum, he was able to indulge to the full his delight in Wagner, and to read copiously, though, it seemed, to no fixed plan of study, veering from the Wisdom of the East to Schopenhauer, from history to mysticism, from Dickens to Dostoevsky, from Yeats to Henry James. Whether Miss McArdle acted on her own initiative, or whether she had been instructed by Mr de Valera to keep an eye on the young man I would not know. He also had regular visits from members of the Starkie family.

In his second year in Dundrum – some time in 1937, I think in the summer, when conditions might have been most favourable, thanks to the long days – and no doubt following the crushing of his hopes of an early release as a result of the Presidential issue – he attempted to escape from the asylum. Indeed, he actually got beyond the high walls surrounding the place. There was complicity from outside: some wealthy Dublin friends, including, most uncharacteristically, a *girl*, who had a crush on him, whom I did not know. The escape vehicle was a large open roadster painted green. The plan was to have him driven to a nearby bay, where a fast motor-boat would whisk him across the Irish Channel. I don't know what was supposed to happen after that. But the attempt failed miserably; I think there was a tip-off, and Edward was picked up less than a quarter of a mile from the asylum. As with so many things in which my friend had been involved, directly or indirectly, the operation had been very badly planned and the security had been non-existent; Edward had even boasted, while at meals, to some of the other inmates, that he would soon be out, and that he would be sending them postcards from Morocco. The whole sequence: the open car painted green, the fast motor-boat lurking at anchor inshore, its light sending out a coded message in response to the regular flashes from a torch from the top of the cliff, had the air of a fairly typical piece of Edwardian – personal not period – melodrama. I remember asking him in Paris, when we met so long after this botched-up affair, whether he had been wearing a red silk *foulard* round his neck, under his white open-necked shirt, and he told me, yes, he had. How did I know? I said that I had guessed that it would be the finishing touch to the full Mark One Escape Outfit.

To return, a moment, to the circumstances of the murder. I think

Edward had acted in a sudden uncontrollable rage, and under pretty severe provocation, even by his mother's standards. He had gone to see his mother that wet, gusty afternoon in mid-February to ask her for an urgent loan – £50 or £60 – that would cover his expenses from Dublin to Cairo. The Gate Theatre was going on an Egyptian tour to put on a series of plays, and Mr Hilton Edwards had offered Edward – or maybe Edward had *thought* that he had made such an offer – a stand-in part, but had made it clear that he would have to provide his own travel expenses. Edward had easily managed to convince himself that this was the chance of a lifetime and that he was at last on the brink of a brilliant career as an actor. But his mother had told him baldly that he would never be any good as an actor, or indeed as anything else, that he had no talent, that he was lazy and uncultivated, that he was incapable of ever seeing anything through to the end, that she had no intention of wasting any more of her money on him, that she had much better things to do with it, that she was going to buy a new car, and perhaps a holiday cottage in Galway, and that she thought she might make a trip to the United States and look up some of her relatives there. According to Edward, after listening to her quite composedly, he had asked her: 'Is that your last word?' And when she had said that it was indeed, and that he was wasting his time and hers, he had gone through the kitchen, opened the back door, gone down to the tool-shed at the bottom of the garden and had fetched the hatchet, had come back into the drawing-room and, in his own words to me, 'let her have it', hacking wildly at any part of her that had come into his range, pursuing her up the stairs, bringing the hatchet down on her arms as she had attempted to protect her head and finishing her off in her bedroom. One of the Directors of Aer Lingus, who had been a young barrister at the time of the trial which he had attended as a junior counsel, told me over dinner at the Stephen's Green Club many years later, that her screams could be heard down the length of St Helen's Road, and that nobody had done anything about it; he said that this was what had horrified him most in the course of the whole trial.

It was perhaps the first time that I had ever felt something approaching compassion for his mother, Medea no longer, a human being horribly battered to death. Edward told me that her last words had been: 'Jesus Maria', adding that, when he had realised that she was dead, he had felt no remorse, there had been no forgiveness in his heart, but he had been seized by a feeling of sheer terror, as if he had had a load of ice cubes in his lower abdomen, with the realisation, as it spread upwards, that he was now a *matricide*, repeating the terrible word to himself so as to allow its full, awful significance to sink into his awareness. He said that this had been the worst moment. It had had nothing to do with any pity for his dead mother, just panic fear for himself. What would happen to him? What was he to do next? The need for immediate action had come almost as a relief. His account filled me with horror. I could not have stood any more. But I was convinced that this was how it must have happened, though it was quite incompatible with his subsequent insistence on premeditation and planning. How could anyone have *planned* such a piece of suburban butchery?

Once he had got over this part of the story he became calmer, even occasionally bursting out into one of his helpless and infectious fits of laughter. His main thought had been that he must somehow dispose of the body. He had gone to the garage and backed the car, the small Baby Austin, into the short drive. It had been as dark as pitch by then, a black, windy night. He had then wrapped the body up in a large plaid rug, carried it downstairs with some difficulty, nearly tripping up halfway down, and had eventually wedged it between the floor and the back seat of the car. He had then headed for the coast, after first doing a detour through central Dublin. In Grafton Street, a little before the bridge over the Liffey, he had run out of petrol, and, getting out, had started pushing the car from the side, holding on to the steering-wheel to guide it forward, in the direction of a petrol station that he knew about and that was near the central post office in O'Connell Street. Fortunately it had been such a filthy night that there had been few people about; but a passer-by – Edward had thought he might have been rather drunk, he had not been walking very straight – seeing his predicament, had come up, offering his help. Edward had got back into the driver's seat, while his helper had pushed the car from behind. It had been heavy going, but the man had managed to make steady progress in the direction of the pump.

At this point of the story, Edward paused, making one of those comments that were both irresistibly and, I think, quite unconsciously, funny: 'There I was, Richard, in the middle of O'Connell Street, with Medea (she had become that again at this stage, now that she was safely dead) wrapped up in the back. It was a bit embarrassing, don't you see? I kept on thinking the chap would see the big bundle through the back window; it was sticking up at that level, and the street-lighting is bright in that part of Dublin. I thought he is bound to want to know what was in it, and it would have been rather awkward if he had started to look' (it would indeed). But the man had expressed no interest; perhaps he had not even noticed the large bundle. When they had reached the pump, he had merely wished Edward better luck for the rest of the journey, and had made off in the dark, after Edward had thanked him rather hurriedly. 'Well, I had got into quite a sweat, anyone would have, right in the middle of O'Connell Street, too'. I suppose they would have, but I could not help feeling that few people would have found themselves in a situation similar to that of Edward on that particular night. It was not exactly an everyday occurrence for one to find oneself transporting the body of one's murdered mother through the centre of Dublin.

Part of my friend's undoubted charm – to myself at least – was his quite startling inability to see anything from anyone else's point of view and his rather endearing tendency to relate everything to his own particular experience. It lent him a sort of naïveté that was as spontaneous as it was irresistible. One might have thought, from his account of that part of the journey, and from his comments on his momentary feeling of embarrassment in the presence of his helper, that it was the most normal thing in the world to have been engaged in this line of transport, that indeed it might have been tendered out to a regular firm of body-carriers so as to insure greater efficiency and celerity. As he had been driving the body of his mother through the city and in the direction of the coast, other people must often have been engaged on similar expeditions. He seemed to put the little bit of bad luck: running out of petrol at some distance from the nearest pump, at exactly the same level of everyday banality as the purpose of this night-time journey across the dark city.

That was the way his mind worked. He wanted other people to share in the uniqueness of his experience, he wanted *me* to. Well, would I not have been a bit embarrassed in similar circumstances, he seemed to say? I had to admit that I supposed that I would have been. It would have been quite useless to have tried to point out to him that it was highly unlikely that I should ever have found myself faced with this sort of problem, that, in any case, I could not drive (he would have argued that I only had to learn). I am quite sure that he was not consciously trying to be funny, though, of course, the effect of such asides, at least on myself, was to send me into convulsions of mirth. This convinced Edward that what he had said had been hilarious; and he was soon equally convulsed. I think, too, we were both glad to have got past the dreadful St Helen's Road bit; the journey after that, whether uphill or downhill, accident-fraught or plain-sailing, could acquire, by comparison with such sheer horror, a levity that was in no way insulting to the poor victim, now indeed merely a rather large bundle hidden in a blanket and filling up much of the back of the little car.

His tank full, Edward had taken the road to the coast, following it to the terminus of the tram route from which we had set off on the walk that had resulted in my summary expulsion from Booterstown. From there he had taken a dirt road the borders of which he had been able to pick out with his lowered headlights, following it till it had petered out at a point from which spread several indistinct paths, indicated by a slight lowering of the level of the coarse grass. He had got out of the car, taking a large torch to guide him, walking in his blue suit and thin city shoes bareheaded in the driving rain – he had left St Helen's Road so hurriedly that he had not even paused to pick up an overcoat, a cap or an umbrella (which would have been quite useless in the howling gale), following first one path, then another, then a third, leaving on the headlights of the car as a beacon to guide him back through the murk to his point of departure. He had thoroughly explored the terrain in the course of his summer walks in search of prospective picnic sites. It was not the sort of place anyone would be likely to come to late on a black and rainy February night. He had now found what he had been looking for, had got back into the car, and had driven very slowly over the bumpy turf in the general direction of the cliffs at a point where they were at their steepest, and from which there was a sheer drop of forty or fifty feet to the jagged rocks below.

He had not gone very far when, to his dismay and consternation, he had seen, in the pitch blackness immediately ahead, a red blur: the rear lights of a stationary car. He told me, years later, that his first reaction at this sight had been one of utter terror, that he had frozen with panic fear. He thought that the police had somehow obtained advance notice of his intentions, and had got there first, and that the *gardai* had been blocking his way forward to the edge of the cliff, in order to catch him red-handed with the bodily evidence of his crime in the back of the car. Then, on thinking it over, and having calmed down a bit, he had realised that this would have been impossible. The car ahead could have nothing to do with the police. He must pull himself together and think out the next step. It was still important that he should not draw attention to his own presence in this unlikely spot – though, with the wind full up, it would have been impossible for anyone to have heard him. Not daring to go into reverse, he had switched off the engine, and had sat down to wait, getting colder and colder. The wait had been agonisingly long: one hour, two hours, three hours, and the red blur had still not moved. In the end, unable to bear it any longer he had ended up by getting out of the car, and, taking the torch once more, and walking on his toes with the caution of a cat, he had stealthily approached the back of the car blocking his way ahead. I can still hear his tone of indignation and outrage when, getting quite red in the face at the evocation of the scene even after fourteen years, he told me, in the Paris restaurant, what his torch had revealed: 'Could you believe it, Richard? There they were, two people, a man and a woman, on the backseat, copulating! absolute animals!' Even after all those years, he still burst with indignation about what he had seen. I burst out laughing, but, for once, he did not join me, his anger still fired at the thought of the distant outrage. I tried gently, between fits of uncontrollable laughter, to point out that the couple could not have known that behind them there was a driver with more urgent priorities. Could he not have some sense of proportion? Of course, he could not. He would not hear of it: copulation was disgusting in any case, and, in this instance, it was holding him up. I had witnessed previous examples of my friend's moral indignation, he could be quite puritanical, the very notion of copulation disturbed him deeply. He tended to treat it as some sort of theoretical notion. I don't think he knew very much about it, he would not have been so indignant if he had.

He had gone back to his car, his clothes by now sopping wet, to resume his vigil, seething with rage and frustration. The couple were certainly having quite a night of it. Eventually, at a bit after three in the morning – and Edward had been worrying about the possibility of being caught where he was at first light, so this came as some sort of a relief – the red blur had started cautiously to move away, had disappeared, and then, over to his right, he had been able to make out the pale headlights of the car as it groped its way back towards the dirt road. At last he could get on with what he had come for. Starting the car, he had driven very cautiously along the vague path to a point at which the blackness of the night had seemed blacker than ever. Getting out and scouting the terrain, he had felt the peaty turf sloping quite sharply beneath his feet which had started slipping in the wet. This was the place all right, even a little beyond it. He had found himself on the very lip of the cliff as it started to curl downward, and had only managed to right himself by holding onto an obtruding root and pulling himself back onto the grassy level. Sweat had been once more pouring down his forehead, temporarily obscuring his eyes and making the night seem more impenetrable and more treacherous than ever. In Paris, at the evocation of his near-slip, his old jaunty sense of fun returned: 'It would have been a bit silly, wouldn't it, Richard, if I had gone over the cliff and Medea and the car had stayed on the top?' And he laughed heartily at the thought of his mother's posthumous revenge. At the time, he had been extra-cautious. There could be no question of driving the car any closer, it would have been too risky: he could himself have been carried away inside it (more chuckles, over the restaurant table, at this thought: 'Medea and I *and* the car would all have gone down together.') So, releasing the hand-brake, he had pushed the car gently from behind. It had soon gathered momentum, swerving a bit to the left. At first he had thought that that was it, that they had both gone over, the car with Medea in it, the ideal solution; that he had not heard the crash below, as they hit the rocks, because it was too far down, and there was too much gale. But then, again to his dismay, not to say horror, he could pick out the pale outline of the Baby Austin – it was painted a light grey – a little to the left of the rim which he had so nearly gone over. Climbing down very gingerly, holding onto roots sticking out of the soil, he had reached the car, which he had found firmly wedged by the bonnet, the front wheels and the axle between two thick branches of a windswept overhanging tree. He had tried dislodging the car by shaking it from side to side from behind, but it would not budge, the damned thing would not budge. On the contrary, the more he pushed it this side and that, the more firmly it became wedged, as if caught in a vice. There had already been a very faint glimmer coming from out to sea, a filthy February dawn was beginning to make a timid washed-out, yellowish appearance. He had soon to get moving. With the courage of desperation, he had managed to climb level with the door to the front passenger seat on the left side. Pulling the seat forward, he had got hold of his mother's body under the armpits, and she had become disengaged from the rug. Luckily, he had not been able to pick out any of the details, it had still been too dark: there was some mercy in that, there had been little enough mercy about the rest of the night. Once out of the car, he had rolled the body down the slope and it had disappeared in the black. He had been about to go, but, on second thoughts, had returned to the car to get the rug, which, caught by the wind, had blown up like a sail, at one moment covering his head, so that he had had to wrestle with it, as if it had been an adversary. He told me how frightened he had been: it was as if the wretched thing had suddenly been endowed with a life of its own. But he had managed to disengage himself from its enveloping folds; and he had watched it, a slight greyness amidst the prevailing black, as it had floated downwards, like a huge, clumsy bird. It had looked to him as if it had indeed followed the body of his mother, unless it had got entangled on the way down. By then he had been past caring. He had wiped his hands on the wet grass – they had become sticky with congealed blood – he had taken the torch and headed inland, walking through the ceaseless rain and the pallid dawn.

He had turned up, sodden, dishevelled, his shoes squelching with water, his clothes torn and covered in traces of chalk and dark stains, at a friend's house, at seven in the morning, asking for a bath and a complete change of clothing, and for something to eat, saying that he was absolutely ravenous. And he had no doubt looked it. He had wolfed down an enormous breakfast: five rashers, three eggs, four sausages, tomatoes, beans, fried bread, followed by toast and marmalade, washed down by three large cups of black coffee. He told me in Paris that he had never enjoyed a meal so much. Then he had taken an early tram to Booterstown. All he had said to his friends was that he had had a bit of a night of it. He certainly had.

He got back to St Helen's Road in time to tell his mother's maid, when she came at nine, that she would not be needed, as his mother had gone away for a fortnight to her friends in Galway. He took care not to let the maid into the hall. He had said that his mother would let her know as soon as she was back, and had given her a fortnight's wages in advance. After the maid had gone, Edward had undressed and gone to bed, sleeping like a stone, and waking up feeling refreshed, and once more very hungry, as if he had just been on a route march. At the moment of awakening, he had felt quite unconcerned, and rather pleased with life. Then, all at once, it had all come back to him, the full horror, the thought of his mother's bedroom, and he had been filled with a hopeless dread, something physical coming up from the pit of his stomach. He had made a feeble attempt to clean the place up, but, seeing that his efforts had only made things worse when he had tried washing the walls – the stains had only come out darker – he had soon given up, apart from boiling some water and washing the hatchet in it. The next few days, he had stayed on at St Helen's Road, only going out to do a little shopping or to visit friends. He had made no attempt to get out of the country though the mailboat was so close; the idea had not even occurred to him. Very soon he had noticed that every time he went out, he was being followed; the men made no attempt to hide themselves. Various people had rung up to enquire about his mother; they had read about her disappearance in the papers. He had followed the same line with them as with the maid: how she did things on the spur of the moment, that he had found a note from her in which she had said that she had decided that she needed a change. On the third day there had been reports of the car having been found. After that, it would only be a matter of time. He had lost all energy, had just felt incapable of movement or decision. He had just stuck on in the little, suburban, blood-stained murder house.

10

Picking up the Bits

Once he was settled in Dundrum, Edward started again to write me regular letters; they were always written on lined, institutional notepaper, yellowish and of poor quality, each sheet of which was topped by an embossed harp, so that, if the letter were long – it generally was – there would be quite a bulge, formed by the half-dozen or so superimposed harps, on the top or bottom half of the envelope. The protuberance of the bulge – or paper bunion – would be a rough gauge of the length of the missive inside. The paper looked as if it had been meant for some schoolboy exercise: a dictation, the horrors of Latin verse; and this impression was reinforced by Edward's cramped handwriting, sloping and unformed. It has not changed at all since then. If the letter had come from an unknown sender, it would have been the sort of handwriting that might have caused a slight tinge of alarm in the addressee, when confronted with the grubby-looking envelope: an anonymous letter or something of the sort, mean and nasty. But it did not inspire any alarm in me. I knew exactly what would be in it.

He wrote to me once a week, his letters always reaching me first post on a Wednesday. I have always liked things to be regular and have generally derived a sense of reassurance from habit and continuity. But I did not look forward to Wednesdays. There was a sort of dull insistence in the presence of the Eire-franked letter beside my breakfast plate of cereals – the bacon and eggs and sausage and tomato would be under a cover in the grate in front of a blazing coal fire – each Wednesday morning. Sometimes it would be hiding beneath a pile of other envelopes and papers, so I would not always spot Edward's letter right away; but, week after week, it was always there, whether sheltering coyly towards the bottom of the pile or brazening it out on the top. I suspected that my scout, who could read my innermost thoughts, and who no doubt regarded me as an awful ass, would vary its position, in a little silent game played with me at a distance. I would note its presence with a mute inward groan and I actually began to regard it as in some way intrusive and vaguely reproachful. Then, one Wednesday, it wasn't there. And its absence continued for the next six or seven Wednesdays. I felt a certain relief, nothing as positive as elation, but as if a rather tiresome link had at last been snapped, and I had regained my freedom from the childish handwriting and the ominous printed Celtic letters. But then, on the seventh or the eighth Wednesday, my little breakfast companion was back – my scout had put it on the top of the pile – fatter than usual, as if its holiday had been put to good physical effect and it had benefited from the long period of rest. In the first letter, there was no reference to the previous silence, no explanation of the sudden and quite unprecedented gap. Nor was there subsequently. It was only when I met Edward in Paris that I learnt that one of the punishments that had been inflicted on him as a result of the attempted escape had been the temporary stoppage of all his mail, both in-going and out-going.

For him the punishment must have come as a severe deprivation, for writing to me was clearly high up among his weekly activities, something that could no doubt be looked forward to, and that helped fill his Sundays and Mondays. He wrote to me with a sort of dogged intent; he wanted to convince me that he was leading quite an enjoyable, even profitable, existence. This was the latest version of the old, only too familiar, Edward Act, addressed, I believe, as much to himself, as to his chosen correspondent. If he repeated often enough that his life was enjoyable and interesting, then perhaps it would indeed become both. He would go into minute, and, to me, rather boring, details about what he had been reading in the course of the previous week, and what he would be reading in the week to come. It was only too clear that he wanted me to keep abreast of his progress, or what he liked to believe was his progress. It was obvious from the start that I had been assigned the role of an extra-mural (in the literal, as well as in the educational, sense; for it had only been during the days of the negotiations between the Chief Inspector and my law tutor, that I had been confined within the walls of Merton) and corresponding tutor, to whom he felt it was his duty to make weekly reports.

I suppose he had other correspondents to whom he had assigned less didactic tasks. There was probably a music tutor somewhere, doubling up no doubt as an operatic one. There may also have been a religious one, inter-denominational and pantheistic, a pot-pourri of the Buddha and the Lord Krishna. Perhaps to some correspondents, male (or even female), he addressed ardent letters of love and passion. Like the letters addressed to myself, these would be read – and no doubt appreciated – twice: first by the asylum authorities, then by the addressee. The love letters, if indeed there were any, may have been directed as much *at* the asylum authorities, in order to titillate their imagination – I would not put it past Edward, and, at our house at Shrewsbury, we had both acquired valuable skills in this branch of the epistolary form, inserting messages in our letters to our parents that were really for the little reptilian eyes of Ferret-Face; and they must have been suffering almost as much from the dull monotony of ordered days as their inmates – as to the recipients of such hot-breathed confessions and molten outpourings. Certainly, they cannot have derived much satisfaction from reading the letters addressed to me.

Week by week, year by year, I received my weekly essay. In 1940 and 1941 the essays sought me out with the Poles in Blackpool and the Czechs in Wilmslow; in 1942, they tracked me down to South

Wales District in Newport and Abergavenny; in 1943, they caught up with me with the Czechoslovak Independent Brigade Group in Hemingford Abbots; in 1944 they managed to penetrate a sealed camp somewhere near the West India Docks, then they followed me to Normandy and beyond, to Roubaix in 1944, to Brussels, to Iserlöhn. Events might move on, huge armies might clash, the future of Europe might hang in the balance, Hitler might shoot himself in his bunker, but the harped letters would still track me down. It must have been harder going for the asylum authorities, concerned, no doubt, to read with care, even *between* the ruled black lines, concerned not to skip anything, in case a hidden message had been wrapped up in some innocent-looking phrase or aside. For I at least could allow myself the small luxury of a good deal of skipping. I am afraid I did not live up to the role that he had intended for me, glad though I was that at least it had not been a more intimate one. There was no call on any reciprocity, no question of shared secrets. My role was to provide my unfortunate friend with a regular mental therapy, a mirror held up to him and in which he could contemplate his intellectual excursions. But his literary and philosophical enthusiasms – always intense, always single-minded, but quickly changing – failed to arouse in me very much interest. In 1937 I was in my second year as an undergraduate and found less and less time or inclination for any sort of extra-mural activity, whether to go to South Wales to help unemployed miners to dig their allotments – the rather patronising vacation pursuit undertaken by some of my more high-minded contemporaries – or attempting closely to follow my friend's most recent preoccupations. So there was the usual discrepancy in our relationship, only it was getting wider and wider. Edward, poor thing, was in desperate need of a witness to his intellectual concerns, and I was a very unwilling, grudging and unsatisfactory one. I too had essays to write – two a week – and I had to read them to people I could *see*; they would make comments on them on the spot. I am afraid I read the lined harped letters hastily and impatiently. Some of them remained unopened, especially after the vacation, when I would come back to my college to find a little pile of them lying uncomfortably on top of one another, toppling this way or that on their bunions, and waiting for me in mute, yet expressive reproach. There they would be, one for each week of the vacation, though the bunions might have caused some of them to fall out of their chronological order. I got bored, even fed up, with the repetitive appeals for attention; I knew what would be in them even before I opened them.

I replied to the fat letters irregularly and cursorily, once a month or every six weeks, and, when in Paris, not at all. I did not tell him very much in my replies. I was very busy, but it seemed indecent to list my activities, which were becoming increasingly varied, to one who had so few; to refer to my travels to one who was perforce immobile; or to talk about my new friends to one who was permanently stuck with a few old ones and who had to make do with a very limited number of regular visitors, whether friends who came to see him, or observers who came to report back on his condition and state of mind. I confined myself to very general expressions of goodwill and vague encouragement: he seemed to be reading some interesting books; why did he not take up a course in Russian, it would be a unique opportunity, with so much time on his hands, and would it not be so much better to read Pushkin in the original? Or, why, then, did he not read Proust in the original French? I did not want to get clear away; after all, we had had some very good moments, had enjoyed some very good laughs at the expense of Ferret-Face, the oily chaplain and the naive and pious Madame Roussel. But Moloch and Medea could not readily be accommodated in a prison-to-college–college-to-prison twice-read correspondence; and, in any case, Edward's mother was hardly a suitable subject of discussion or reminiscence, while his father had become a somewhat distant figure, and one whom I had never actually met. And I could think of little else to talk about; even the changing sky or the view of Merton Grove in winter as seen from my far window would have been a little unfair. I felt instinctively that landscape was a forbidden topic, if only because it moved and unfolded. There was no point in reminding Edward that I could command an almost limitless range of vision, that I was free to cycle as far as my legs would take me, or that I could jump on a bus without looking at its destination, just to see where it would take me to. It would have been inconsiderate thus to have reminded him that there was always a beyond, and another one beyond that. 'Beyond' was a word to be avoided. It was like trying to write to someone who was deprived of one of the essential faculties. In fact there was so much that I could not talk about. In so far as I gave any thought to it, it was a pretty unsatisfactory situation. I could have tried harder, no doubt; but I was busy, moderately happy, and constantly excited by new experiences and new discoveries. I had all the selfishness of twenty. Dundrum was quite unreal to me; I could not picture it at all; it was just the place where all those harped letters came from.

But I was very interested in just what had happened to land him where he was, and wanted to find out more. There seemed to be so many unanswered questions, and I knew so little about the exact sequence of events that had all at once led up to the murder. I was quite unconvinced by my friend's repeated assertions that it had all been carefully planned and premeditated. This – like so much else – was clearly complete fantasy, at least a rearrangement of events from the far side of their completion. Edward must have acted on a sudden impulse. But what had that been? What had finally pushed him over? It was not a morbid interest; indeed I tried to give as little thought as possible to what had happened in No. 23. It was like a piece of research not yet completed. I felt that I had to find out more, that I must know the epilogue of a silly schoolboy story so many of the chapters of which we had written jointly, even if, at the outset, I had stepped into the story halfway through, without having had the opportunity of reading the previous chapters. It wasn't just the epilogue that had to be filled in. I had missed at least a couple of chapters at the far end, those that had covered the period of a year or so that Edward had spent in Dublin after leaving Shrewsbury.

Why had he gone back to Dublin? If only he had kept away from the place, had buried himself in the vastness of London or the anonymity of some other big city, he might have led a normal life, the irreparable would have been avoided. I knew Edward well enough to have realised, even after I had met Brian Inglis on that February morning, that he was not a natural killer, that anyone, other than his mother, would have been quite safe with him. Returning to Dublin had been the fatal mistake; everything had followed from this decision. But Edward was naturally gregarious, always in need of a wide audience of friends and admirers, he was not the sort of person to have thought of burying himself in some vast metropolitan sprawl in which he did not know – and was not known to – anyone. He did not share my taste for a lonely boarding-house existence, the timid company of strangers, the marvellous freedom of solitude; even the promiscuity of an English public school had not given him a lingering taste for his own company. Besides, he liked his comforts; he was luxury-loving and would have been horrified by the sort of conditions I was quite prepared to put up with. I don't think he had had a happy childhood, but it seemed to have been a rich one. In Dublin, money would have been more readily available than elsewhere; there were plenty of people he could have borrowed from if it were a matter of tiding him over a difficult period of waiting; and he had come away from school with the bare minimum of qualifications. Finally Dublin was his home, had always been. I had realised, from his eagerness as my guide, that he was quite proud of the city, a place in which his family had played a prominent civic part.

So I don't suppose that he ever thought of an alternative course of action. Anyhow, he went back to Dublin. In Dublin he was trapped in a whole series of roles that he would have difficulty in avoiding. There was, first of all, the part assigned to him, or that he had assumed, in the impossible family scene. And there existed an extensive audience of friends that had to be played up to and that might provide the applause. I knew nothing, or hardly anything, about this faithful audience, save that it no doubt provoked in Edward even more extravagant responses than those prompted by the captive, almost immobile audience of the members of our house at Shrewsbury. Back in Dublin, he enjoyed full freedom of movement; he was no longer a schoolboy, and if there was a less insistent need to provoke, there would be a greater one to astonish. He would now command a wider stage, though not all that much wider. From my single visit I had come away with the impression that it was a city in which one would meet the same people again and again, perhaps in the course of a single day. Of course, this was equally true of my home town, Tunbridge Wells. But the Royal Borough offered no stimulus to extremes, to ostentation. It called on all performers to maintain a low key; it favoured muted colours and the unwritten rules of a discreet conduct. It would have been difficult to have associated the Wells with violence; or it would have been discreet, soft-walking, stockinged violence, behind closed curtains, arsenic perhaps. Dublin, as far as I could make out, put a positive premium on high drama, on exaggeration; a recent violent history was never very far away, and people in costume, in fancy-dress, walked its streets.

I had remembered from my first visit the startling figure of Maude Gonne McBride in her long green cloak with its embroidered golden harp over her heart. She was not just a monument, nor just a familiar, rather eccentric figure, but a bit of both, on display at certain hours of each day on St Stephen's Green. The place seemed to be cluttered with monuments – living, long since dead, and recently dead. Later, I wondered at the sheer banality of the little third-class hotels and lodging-houses in which the officers of British Intelligence had been murdered, in some cases in bed with their wives, early in the morning of Bloody Sunday. I marvelled, too, at the Victorian comfort and dowdiness of the big house – it might have been in Broadwater Down, in Tunbridge Wells, in monkey-puzzle-land – in which Patrick Pearse had housed his school. Many years later, I was being driven by a pupil of mine along a canal somewhere near one of Dublin's cemeteries. We were passing a row of mean-looking houses; he pointed to one, commenting: 'During the troubles, the IRA used to torture people there.' A down-trodden, down-at-heel sort of violence in suitable premises, or martyrs' careers emanating from big Victorian houses half-hidden among yews and thick evergreens – I found it an odd and architecturally most uninspiring mixture, almost as vulgar as the dreadful, brightly painted Catholic parish churches.

Then there was the peculiar topography of the place: a capital with Georgian city squares and a series of seaside outlying districts, the huge crescent of the sweeping bay, the nearness of the blue hills to the south and west, quite wild empty country, with a scattering of ruined, windowless, roofless barracks, their walls still bearing the traces of fire, lapping at the edges of banal, beige-coloured suburbs, a city that it was quite easy to walk out of. I felt that if I were to understand what had happened to Edward since I had last seen him at that brief meeting in Kensington – an occasion marked by our usual juvenile frivolity – I would have to go to Dublin, not in order to go over the ground, to walk to the sea at Shankill and look over, or anything so literal and so morbid as that. I had no intention of taking another look at St Helen's Road, nor of following the murder trail from there. But I wanted to take in the place on its own terms. On my first visit, Edward had been a constant, insistent, and thoughtful guide and companion; he had wanted me to see the sights, but I had not had the opportunity to wander off on my own. I had barely taken in the evidence of extreme poverty. We had taken public transport everywhere, or Edward had driven me in a friend's open car, so that I had gained few notions of how one quarter related to another, or why there were so many vast Anglican churches in places like Kingstown and Rathmines.

So I felt that the first thing I must do was to return to Dublin on my own and to take in the city slowly, bit by bit, on foot. The place might also provide me with some of the answers – I had spent so little time with Edward on his home ground – and there were two people I particularly wanted to see: Michael Feeney, the former warder of the Mountjoy, who now worked for a private lunatic asylum in Surrey called the Flower House, but who had told me that, in the summer, he would be on holiday at his parents' place near Dublin; Cyril Monson, the actor at the Gate, who had shared the Upper Mount Street flat with Edward. I might even try and beard the redoubtable Miley & Miley (would they both be there? which would speak first?); there was not much that they could do to me now, save refuse to see me. I thought that I might well approach Madame Roussel; there was no one else in my friend's family that I could think of. I might even try and get permission to visit Edward in Dundrum, but this seemed a very long shot; as I was not a relative, I did not think I would be granted it (I wasn't). This did not worry me. I wanted to explore the terrain, get my bearings, find out things for myself, establish a relationship with the city, as if I were part of it, talk to people in pubs, listen to people talking in pubs, watch the crowds in the parks or at race meetings up in the hills, test the feeling of the hourly and the weekly calendar of movement, compare Monday to Friday, experience the extra bustle, in peripheral areas, of Saturday, wake up to the quiet of Sunday. It wasn't a post mortem or anything of that kind. It might not even help me very much with Edward; but it could turn out to be quite an agreeable holiday in an unfamiliar urban environment.

So I went to Dublin in July 1938, after I had had my last viva (I had five in the course of two successive days). I cannot remember now just where I stayed, but it must have been in a cheap boarding-house, probably in the area beyond the Castle. It was certainly a very poor area, for it teemed with quite cheerful children, most of them shoeless, all of them ragged, with very dirty legs, and faces that grinned beneath the grime. There were women in large shawls sitting on doorsteps holding their babies; this seemed to be a silent way of begging, because they congregated on the steps of churches. I do remember, too, that at certain improbable hours of the day there would be long queues of men in cloth caps, battered trilbies or bowlers, their hands in their pockets, bending down every now and then to spit on the ground while avoiding their feet, standing outside the pubs, waiting for them to open. Altogether, especially in the areas of the Castle and the Four Courts, there seemed to be a lot of men about, just standing, a lot of women about, just sitting. And every-where in this part of the city there were children on the move, fast, running in tight clusters or spread out in loose formations, shouting and making a lot of cheerful noise. I had never seen a place so full of children.

I had written in advance both to Cyril Monson and to Michael Feeney, asking if I could see them, explaining to the former that I was a schoolfriend of his one-time flat-mate. I had a friendly reply from Feeney, saying that he would be delighted to see me, adding that, from our previous correspondence, he had had the feeling that he already knew me, and would do whatever he could to make my stay in Dublin enjoyable. This had seemed decidedly promising, and I had to admit to myself that enjoyment was not entirely alien to the stated purpose of my trip. Cyril Monson had replied rather guardedly that he would be willing to see me if he could find the time between rehearsals – the Gate was putting on a new show in the autumn – adding that he did not think he could be of very much help, but suggesting that I get in touch with him once I was in Dublin. This I did the day after my arrival. He invited me round to his top-floor flat for a drink at six that evening. When I turned up, I was greeted by a very good-looking man, dark, rather sallow, with thick hair parted at the side, elegant in a slightly over-dressed way, in a three-piece suit, his gold cufflinks obtruding, as if anxious to be seen, from his blue and white striped cuffs. He looked about thirty, but he might have been older; at twenty, I was no judge of such things. The flat was neat, spotless and well cared for. There were tiny articles of furniture that looked valuable; the table tops shone with polish, and on the walls there were black-framed prints of Japanese warriors, wrestlers and scantily dressed ladies holding sunshades. He looked as if he had been given the right Christian name and had spent the rest of his life living up to it. He was very polite in a stiff way and articulated clearly; one could even pick out the *-ed* of verbs in the past tense.

At first he seemed slightly ill at ease, as if awaiting questions that might be too probing; and he took a long time with his back to me, preparing drinks for the two of us in front of a corner-cupboard, as if to gain time further to compose himself. But as I kept off the subject of the murder, refraining from asking him if it had come as a surprise and a shock to him, and as I did not question him at all about his relationship with Edward, how they had met originally, whether they had had shared interests, he brightened up and seemed much more relaxed. I told him that the main purpose of my visit was to ask him what he thought of Edward as an actor. He grinned broadly at this, adding that, if I knew Edward as well as he supposed I did – for I had known him much longer than he had – I would know the answer: he was absolutely *hopeless*, would never have made even an actor on provincial rep, with however much training; he totally lacked the imagination to project himself into a new, unfamiliar personality. I asked him if he had ever told our friend this, if he had tried to persuade him that he had mistaken his vocation and had suggested that he take up something else. No, of course he had done nothing of the kind: it would have been pointless, and he had not wanted to provoke a situation which would have resulted in Edward adopting his high-and-mighty manner and flouncing out in a fury. Looking round the pretty room, he added: 'I have some rather nice pieces, you see.' Having witnessed some of Edward's rages and their effect on any objects that stood within reach, I could appreciate the strength of his objection. Of course he had been absolutely right. Edward was the last person ever to be prepared to listen to something that he did not want to hear. There did not seem much point in pursuing this dismal topic; but he did tell me that Edward had not actually been *offered* a place on the Egyptian tour, but that he had badgered Mr Hilton Edwards so insistently that the director of the Gate had eventually agreed that, if he could provide for his expenses, there was no reason why he should not come along, though he thought he would be throwing away his money.

Before I left, Cyril Monson told me that much of the trouble with Edward during the time that the two of them had shared the flat was that Edward had fallen in with a rather silly set of very well-to-do young people – Dublin's *jeunesse dorée*, he described them, not without affectation (and, so I thought, a hint of jealousy, something I could detect, because I felt something of it myself – these people had been concealed from me). They went around in red sports cars and open green roadsters and had a great deal of money to burn. Edward had been flattered by their interest and by the speedy transition as a result of which he had been accepted as one of their own, putting this down to their social acumen. He had had no difficulty in convincing himself that this was just the manner of life most suited to his own rather flamboyant temperament. I had seen something of this side of him during our schooldays or in the vacation: bawling out a waiter who had been slow to take an order, or a high-handed manner with a taxi-driver, or on the contrary, over-tipping: 'Take this, keep the change.' Now he had made it in the Dublin smart set: a just recognition of his own rightful place in society (Monson commented that it was from this time that Edward had ceased to refer to Dublin as 'a provincial dump'). The trouble, of course, was that these people had a great deal of money to throw away, but that Edward hadn't. Nor did he have any prospect of employment, lucrative or not. Naturally, such mundane matters would not have been discussed in the company of his new friends. He would let them assume that he was a young man of private means who could afford the best tailors in town and who was something of a gourmet. Most of the previous roles that he had taken on had not involved him in any material consequences; they had merely amused his more indulgent friends and had fed, without cost, his own fantasies. But this time he soon began running into trouble, once he had tried keeping up with the extravagant way of life of the fast set by which he had been so readily adopted. His flat-mate thought that he might have borrowed quite a bit, perhaps several hundred. I could see now how the mounting volume of debt might have led very directly to what had happened in St Helen's Road. No doubt his mother had reproached him with his recent extravagance, had suggested that he was attempting to cut a figure among people who could afford what he could not; and this would have been as wounding and as unforgivable as telling him that he had no talent as an actor. From what I had known of his mother I could imagine that she would have let out all the stops, would have mocked his general incapacity, and would have stung him to the quick by suggesting that he was attempting to fly too high. And, knowing Edward even better, I could well appreciate that his memory, always subjected to a saving form of censorship, would have eliminated her more wounding remarks, only to retain her expressed disbelief in his theatrical prospects. I had then gained something from my visit to Upper Mount Street.

Cyril Monson had quite a lot more to say about Edward's new

friends. It was this set of sillies that had made such a mess of the attempted escape the year before. Probably for them it had been just another flirtation with danger, another lark, another effort to escape the boredom of life in a very provincial town, the capital of a peasant country. He added the information that the girl who had been the leading spirit in the escape attempt had been the nineteen-year-old sister of one of the young bloods, that she had had a crush on Edward, as well she might have had, for he was very personable, good-looking in a conventional sort of way, and could be absolutely charming when the situation demanded it.

I could not help feeling resentful at the discovery of the new friends, almost as if Edward had been concealing something from me. I suppose it was the realisation that he had been living on several planes at once, and that he had taken great care to keep each one apart. I had belonged to one plane, his schoolboy infatuations to another, and the new Dublin crowd to yet another. It was natural that he should have been concerned to keep the different sets apart, relating each only to himself. And it was silly of me to have reacted in this way, especially as I had so often found him quite overpowering and much too demanding. Anyhow I found no urge to follow up what Monson had told me and to seek out any of the Dublin group, though no doubt any of them could have filled me in with details of Edward's life which had remained an almost complete blank as far as I was concerned. I cannot really explain this reluctance, save possibly that further enquiry might have revealed my friend as even sillier than I had thought him to be. Also, they sounded a pretty unpleasant lot. It seemed uncharacteristic of Edward that he should have wanted to mix with the sort of people whom I would have found the most antipathetic. Of course I was being completely unreasonable. But I made no effort to fill in the missing chapter. I think Monson must have felt much the same. Anyhow, he shook my hand quite effusively, asking me to come and see him again if I got bored in Dublin. I would be very welcome; and he would like to hear my impressions of his native city. I did not in fact take up his offer.

I met Michael Feeney by arrangement outside the Bank of Ireland at three in the afternoon. In his letter, he had offered to do whatever he could to contribute to the enjoyment of my stay in Dublin. I realised, with some dismay, on meeting him, that he had meant this in a very precise sense. For he was not alone. He introduced me to his companion, a handsome young man with fair curly hair, very bright eyes, rather vacant, tall, with a beautiful figure, and holding himself so well that I thought that there was something professional about his bearing, as though he had taken lessons in standing up (later in the day, I came to the conclusion that he had also taken lessons in walking). Feeney said: 'This is a *very* good friend of mine. His name is Brendan, he is only eighteen, and he is a *garda* in the Dublin City corps', adding, I thought rather inconsequently – I was already puzzled by his apparent need to provide me with this mini-biography of his friend, as if I had been about to employ him in some capacity or other – 'you two should get on very well', at which point he walked off, disappearing into the crowd, leaving the two of us looking at one another in some bewilderment. Well, *I* was certainly bewildered; I had expected a long talk with Feeney about Edward; it was Edward who had first brought the two of us in touch; and he had landed me with this completely unknown young policeman. I did not know what to do, nor what to say. My immediate instinct was to cut and run, it would have been easy enough in the afternoon bustle of this part of central Dublin, and neither the blonde Brendan nor Feeney would have known how to track me down. But it would have been rude, and the young man looked as if he might be easily hurt. Also my curiosity got the better of my prudence: Brendan might have something important to tell me about Edward. He, on the other hand, did not appear to be particularly embarrassed, as if it had been the most natural thing to have been left, virtually without introduction in the company of a complete stranger. I could not help wondering what Feeney had told him about me, how he had prepared him for this bizarre situation, what assignment, if any precise one, he had proposed to him. All I knew was that it could not have been a professional one: my unexpected companion was in civilian clothes, he did not seem to be in a hurry, he was certainly off-duty, and Feeney was no longer in the prison service.

We walked up and down rather purposelessly three or four times in front of the lovely building; I thought it lovely, the eyes of my companion registered no reaction to it. Then Brendan broke the ice by asking me my Christian name, and then suggested that, as it was such a lovely day, Richard, why did we not go for a long walk along the coast, the nice thing about Dublin was that the coast was always within walking distance, and Michael had told him that I was a good walker (as I had only seen Feeney *once*, over tea in a Corner House, I don't know how he could have come by this particular bit of information; but he had a good many other preconceived ideas about me, as I was soon to discover). So we took a tram along a vaguely familiar route; I was glad of this respite, as it gave me time to think about the strange turn of events that had thus landed me sitting next to a young *garda* on the top deck of a Dublin Corporation public vehicle. At least, I thought, he was not likely to expose me to the sort of agonising embarrassment Edward had put me to in a similar location. As we passed each church, Brendan crossed himself with discretion. We did not exchange a word while on the tram.

At the terminus, we set off along a narrow road, till it petered out among chunks of broken paving, covered in weeds. We soon reached the top of the cliffs, following a footpath which seemed to be the one Edward and I had taken on the long walk the evening before my expulsion from Booterstown. We must, at some stage, have passed quite near the spot where Edward's mother had gone over the cliff. Indeed, I thought at one moment, as we skirted the lip of the cliff, that this must be the purpose of our walk; but Brendan kept on along the cliff edge without showing any sign of wanting to stop, so it could not be that; in a way I was relieved. I had not wanted that pointed out to me; but my relief soon gave way to renewed agitation at the thought of my present peculiar predicament. It was a beautiful day, with a pleasant breeze off the sea; and for a time we walked in silence, much to my relief, for I could not think of any subject that might be of shared interest between my unexpected (and willing or unwilling?) companion and myself. So we went on, each looking straight ahead, without saying a word, for a mile or more. But I could now feel the silence rising up between us and distracting us, or at least myself, from the enjoyment of the view. I have always found silence on the part of a companion exceedingly off-putting and my usual reaction to silent people has been to gabble away like an idiot, listening to myself doing so, and becoming more and more aware that, with every new hurried word, I was putting myself at a greater disadvantage. There seemed to be no doubt that the next move was up to me, but I did not know what it should be, I was not even sure what game we were supposed to be engaged in, but some sort of game was going on. There must be some way of breaking the deadlock. I thought I'd try an experimental kite, asking my companion if he liked walking. He said that he did as long as he had a nice friend to walk with, he did not like going on solitary walks. This did not seem to get us very far, the remark might be as harmless as it appeared, or it might have a more precise significance. I tried again: did he ever go out this way with his girl? This time he blushed deeply, looking hurt, before replying that he did not have a girl, as though a girl were some obscene object. In order to smooth him down, I told him that I too did not have a girl, and at once he seemed reassured.

I did not like the way things seemed to be going, but they were certainly going in a pretty precise direction, and it was not the direction I wanted to go in. I began feeling panicky. Somehow, I had got myself into this, or had been got into this, and I could not see how I was decently going to get out of it, there did not seem to be any easy exit. I thought I would try a last throw, if only to gain time and put off the hour of reckoning, which seemed to be approaching at fearsomely implacable speed. I asked Brendan if he had been a friend of Edward's. He looked genuinely puzzled at this, before answering that he did not know anyone called Edward, though he had had a schoolfriend of that name, but that had been some time ago. I tried again: had Michael Feeney told him anything about a friend of mine called Edward? He replied that Michael had never mentioned such a person. We were getting nowhere. It was his turn to look embarrassed.

Then he took the plunge: was I not then a *fairy*, too, he asked; Michael had said that I was, and had suggested that we two might have a good time together, making his point only too clearly by adding that there were plenty of secluded spots a bit further on, hidden glades and green and yellow mossy floors where there was no risk of being disturbed; he had been this way many times before, and knew all the nice spots. So there was nothing for it. I had to admit, and I must have sounded pretty foolish, for I spoke with genuine regret, as if I wished that my answer could have been different, that I *wasn't* a fairy (I hadn't heard the word used before, but it was not difficult to guess its meaning). Then, to make things better, as I thought, I qualified what I had just said by adding that I didn't *think* I was a fairy. This was of course a bad mistake, even though it had been designed only to soften the blow and to maintain a level of politeness in our exchanges. The young policeman did not see it that way, taking my remark as a sign of hesitation; quick to seize the advantage, he pointed out that there was no time like the present, that it was only a matter of taking the first step, that I need not be shy, that he would be very gentle. I was quite terrified by this new turn of events. I had never had sex with anybody else, and did not feel at all inclined to starting on a twosome with an unknown Irishman. I was perhaps young for my age, but at twenty-one, I was as shy of men as I was of girls. This I tried to explain to him as politely as possible, feeling all the time that I was only making matters worse and that I was getting myself in deeper and deeper. Luckily, his reaction to my protestations was one of anger, rather than of pained disappointment. As far as he was concerned, it was clear that there had been no misunderstanding. Why the *hell* then, he went on snappily, had I agreed to come out for a walk with him? Not to admire the beauty of the day, the shimmer of light off the sea, or any bunk of that kind, for sure! In his anger, he had revealed his natural crudeness and vulgarity. I was more anxious than ever to get away from him as fast as possible; and his anger made me bolder.

I suggested a bargain: there had been a misunderstanding, whatever he might have thought, and neither of us was to blame for it. I could appreciate that I had been the indirect cause of his having wasted most of his one afternoon off. Could I not at least compensate him? It seemed only fair that he should not go away empty-handed, after all the trouble that he had been put to. I offered him there and then £5, taking out the notes. He accepted them without the slightest embarrassment, which made me think that he had been in the habit of receiving tips either for similar services, or for favours of another kind, on plenty of previous occasions. I still wondered how we were going to bring to a decorous close this unfortunate social get-together, when he put an abrupt, indeed rather brutal, end to my fears. I had thought that he would insist on accompanying me back, and had presumed that we would have walked on the return journey in painful silence. But he did nothing of the kind. Observing that there did not seem any point in our continuing the walk together, he said that I could find my own way back to Dublin, it was not difficult, I could not go wrong. And then he walked off purposefully and at a brisk pace in the direction we had been going together. I felt immensely relieved, it had been cheap at the price. But I thought too that he was very lacking in manners.

It was not as if Virtue had triumphed, or anything like that. I was just not prepared for casual sex, whether bought or offered free of charge, especially with someone with the Christian name of Brendan. But I think it would have been the same if he had been called something less commonplace. I was very far from innocent, but my lack of innocence was mostly in the mind. I just did not know what men (or, for that matter, a man and a woman) did together, though I suspected that it was not very nice. I could not tell, in consequence, what would have been expected of me in this type of social situation involving two. My unwillingness did not spring from any moral inhibitions, but from a fear of making a fool of myself, of being found out as almost totally ignorant. Also, I found the thought of the whole business somewhat revolting, especially with a young policeman I had only met a few hours earlier. I could see no extra excitement in the opportunity thus offered of 'crossing the barriers of class' (or of nationality), and that sort of thing; and Brendan had appeared coarse and crude, rather than exotic. No doubt I was distressingly normal, though I was not aware of the fact. I was certainly sexually very immature.

My Dublin trip had taken a most peculiar turn. Monson had been helpful and polite, but Feeney had read me wrong. He had done his best for me, according to his lights. He had wanted my stay in Dublin to be enjoyable, and knowing that my old friend in the city was now in a State asylum, and that I might be lonely, he had thoughtfully provided me with a handsome and consenting companion. I suppose I should have been grateful. But all I had felt was extreme embarrassment and immense relief at having got out unscathed from a very awkward situation.

I was not sure where Edward could have fitted into what had turned out a rather disastrous encounter. I had been aware of most of his passionate affairs with younger boys in our House – far from making a secret of them, he had wanted me to know all about them, from the start to the finish (for there was always a finish, sometimes one both sudden and messy). I had put these down to the sort of temporary involvements that so often grew from the very conditions of life in an English Public School, at least among boarders. I had rather supposed that my friend, like so many others, would eventually grow out of them, once removed from a rather abnormal existence. I now began to wonder whether his mother had known of her son's schoolboy inclinations. Knowing her as well as I had, I felt sure that she would have made the most of any weakness or what might be described, in a very provincial society, as abnormality, to make fun of him, particularly in the presence of others. For she had always been at her worst (or, in terms of sheer dramatic performance, at her best) if she and Edward had witnesses to what could hardly have been described as their conversations. Over the years she had developed considerable skills in picking at and probing her son's not very well guarded secret topographies.

Edward would have been unlikely to have told me if his mother had worked on this line of attack – there were areas of reticence in our relations. It would not have been like his telling me that she had gone out of her way to taunt him with his professional incompetence as an actor. Certainly, I had never heard her pursue this particular line of denigration, but those in Dublin closer to him may have had it served up to them. I could not believe that she would have simply let it go for it would have provided yet another weapon in her already formidable armoury (though I suppose it is just possible that, with her convent education, she might simply have been unaware of such schoolboy attachments and what they might have signified). In her relations with her son, she was not an intelligent adversary, being always in too much of a rush and concerned to gain immediate effects. Just as she was liable to throw at him anything at hand –

teapots, cups, glasses, small tables, paperweights, or indeed anything hard, especially if it would splinter, she never hurled cushions – she would be equally improvident with her verbal accusations, provocations or insinuations. She would have been quite unable to hold back to the last what she regarded as likely to be her most telling weapon. In this respect, Edward and his mother had quite a lot in common. He had told me, on our first encounter in Paris, that, at a certain point in the conversation, he had gone down to the bottom of the garden, returned with the chopper, and 'let her have it'. But she too had always 'let him have it' with everything that she could marshall, even if it were a matter of emptying the pockets of his suits and jackets and then showering their contents with joyful abandon over his curly head, letting him have the whole lot, in a paper snow-storm, in one go. Edward had always been careless about what he left around; and he must have received scores of letters from the boy in Eastbourne with whom he had been so deeply involved at school. And there may have been plenty of letters from other boys. She would have named names, would have gone slowly through the full roll-call. I don't think Edward would have liked this, especially if she had accompanied her list of the one-time favourites with threats to tell the parents of the schoolboys whom she had succeeded in identifying. Nor would these have been empty threats. She would have written the letters all right. Her concern to do harm could make her uncharacteristically energetic, though her energies might be misdirected, and she would probably have got some of the addresses wrong; and the *coup*, or series of *coups*, might have misfired, as had been the case with all those letters sent out to the heads of Oxford and Cambridge mens' colleges; the Heads had failed to respond. Some of the parents might not have wanted to know, might have consigned her letters to the waste-paper basket. But no doubt some would have got home.

All this is a very difficult area to explore, if only because, as far as I could make out, Edward and his mother had conducted a very private form of warfare against one another over the course of years. Most of this must have been bottled up between them. But some of it must have spilled over from the mutually accepted terrain of encounter in the drawing-room of No. 23. There must have been some people, especially in Dublin, who had known more about this aspect of the mother-and-son conflict than I ever did. I had been an accidental onlooker of the battle, a temporary war correspondent covering only the fraction of a campaign – perhaps just the opening shots – then quickly dismissed from the scene (so no true chronicler of the First, Second, Third and Fourth Booterstown Wars). I had witnessed a certain number of skirmishes, a few unprovoked aggressions on the part of his mother, but I had missed all the heavy stuff. And I had arrived very late on the scene of conflict. But a few people must have been in on campaign and counter-campaign, offensive and counter-offensive, truce, soon broken, and renewal of hostilities, from the very beginning.

Had there ever existed a loving and affectionate relationship between mother and child? Had that relationship suddenly turned sour, as a result of some particular incident, or had it slowly marinated in mounting mutual rancour? How had she treated him as a baby (there would certainly have been a maid and a nanny to do all the hard work) and as a small boy? When had things started to go wrong, if they had ever been right, between them? Had the decision to send Edward away to boarding-school been taken in order to remove a loathed presence from his mother's home for eight or nine months of the year at least? (And his mother, to my knowledge, had never put any difficulties in the way of Edward's staying with schoolfriends during the holidays.) Normally, if the decision in favour of a boarding-school had been at the instigation of Edward's father, his mother would have opposed it as such; so her agreement must have come from her desire to have him removed to the other side of the Channel. When had his mother become 'Medea' (as she has still remained for her sixty-eight-year-old son in 1983, nearly fifty years after her murder)? Had there been some odd element of affection or amused familiarity in this bestowal of a nickname that had outlasted by so many years the person on whom it had originally been bestowed and that had kept her permanently ageless? For it was hard to take Medea quite seriously and to recognise in her the demon-figure that the nickname was no doubt supposed to suggest. I still find it vaguely comical, a schoolboy joke from a very long time ago. What had originally provoked what, in my time, had become a constant, even stable, state of hostility? Had the initiative in aggression come from his mother? These were all questions that I have never been able to answer. As I have said, Edward never referred to his childhood, save, very occasionally, to talk about his celebrated paternal grandfather, who had been Director of Dublin Zoo, in conversations with myself. So I could not know how, why, or when it had all begun. I had only come in on the last two chapters.

I spent the rest of my stay in Dublin very much on my own, glad of my own company, and pleased enough to be able to explore the city in my own time and at my own pace, without the accompaniment of a guide. I covered a great deal of ground on foot. I was not unhappy, but I did feel a bit lonely much of the time, as well as very alien, something that I had never felt in Paris or anywhere else in France (save Bordeaux). Everything served to remind me that I did not belong in this scene of a recent bloody past – I am not referring to the murder. I even found myself at moments missing Edward's mother and the little house in St Helen's Road, if only because both had been familiar. I had been inside the house; and this time the only house I got inside was Monson's flat. I tried to break down the barrier of loneliness and foreignness by buying and reading a lot of books published by the Talbot Press; and, once, when I was sitting in a large café in O'Connell Street, having tea and reading *Casement's*

Last Adventure, by Captain Monteith, who had been with Casement on the submarine, two oldish men – they seemed oldish to me, but they were probably in their forties – came up to me and stood over me; one of them said: 'Well done, laddie, I am glad to see a young fellow like you reading a really good book, keep on at it.' I had blushed and said nothing, for fear of revealing my English accent. Still, it had been a brief breach in my loneliness. It was the only one.

I did go and see Miley & Miley, who were most unfriendly and very informative. They made it clear that they had been very disappointed that I should have escaped their clutches at the time of the trial. They told me that there was not the slightest likelihood of my obtaining permission to visit Edward in Dundrum. They still seemed genuinely to believe that I had been an evil influence, even *the* evil influence. Let them think so, if that gave them satisfaction, I thought; it did not make any difference to me. I have never liked lawyers, but I did not think any could be so silly. I applied for permission, but it was refused. I returned home via Shrewsbury, where my former history master told me that I had got a Second. It was a great disappointment, but I was still glad to be back in England. I did not return to Dublin till 1962, when I stopped there for a week-end, on my way to Belfast. I went to a French restaurant somewhere near Trinity. Once inside, the place seemed familiar to me; and I remembered that I had been there with Edward during my first stay. It was just the sort of place that he would have patronised. It was still very good.

11

Epilogue

I saw the train come in on the far platform. I would give him time to cross to the near side through the underpass before waiting at the barrier. I had the same feeling of mild curiosity and moderate expectancy that I had experienced that time waiting for the Le Havre train at Saint-Lazare, though I thought that this time we would have less to talk about. I had not seen him for nearly twenty years and wondered what he would be looking like. He had always taken pretty good care of himself, so I expected him to have weathered well. There was no one in the ticket office, and I was just about to take up my place opposite the barrier when I heard a very affable voice from behind me addressing me in more than passable French: '*C'est Monsieur Richard, n'est-ce-pas?*' on a note both enquiring and faintly mock-deferential. (He had taken to closing his letters recently in rather formal, curiously anodyne French salutations: *comme toujours, meilleurs voeux, à très bientôt, meilleures amitiés*, and that sort of thing; I had not been able to make out if these were some sort of leg-pull, or simply his latest way of closing a brief letter.) So he had spotted me first, and was obviously pleased with the effect of surprise. He had arrived on an earlier train, had gone for a walk, taking in the cathedral, and had returned, taking me from the back.

I turned round to take in the presence of a rather stately, slow-moving figure, slightly bent, an elderly gentleman who, with his enlarged very blue eyes peering enquiringly through heavy spectacles, looked a bit like some sort of reddish fish: rather a cautious, largish fish which swam forward with careful deliberation, its eyes like headlights in the deep; various attachments, like fins or aeriels, moving in slow sweeps, like living plants or wispy outgrowths, would not have seemed out of place. His slightly bulbous eyes seemed to be staring, though in a not unfriendly way; the hair was still reddish, but thinning, and the face was very red. It was hard to associate this rather deliberate figure, the very large head beginning to settle into the neck and powerful shoulders, even remotely with what had happened coming up to fifty years back, hard that is, till, in the unmistakable emphatic tone of old, and with the same studied mock deference, he started talking about Moloch and Medea. It was exactly the same agreeable voice, toned to express pleasure, amusement, delight, warmth, and a still juvenile enthusiasm (enthusiasm, I sometimes thought, had been his undoing, causing him to get everything completely out of proportion). It was a voice too that was accompanied, in almost every sentence, by exclamation marks, just as, in his letters, so many sentences terminated in a double exclamation mark. Indeed, one could have taken the stylistic device even further; so much of his life, at least such of it as I had known, could be fitted in front of exclamation marks, single, double, treble, as if in constant amazement and single-minded wonder and enjoyment. The exclamation marks seemed to retain the juvenile qualities of so much else, they also struck me, in these first few minutes, as revealing the old, old desire to impress, to amaze, to shock, even to dazzle. There was no great change there, but still a lingering youthfulness, quite unstudied, and perhaps a still surviving naïveté, both attractive, if (as always) rationed. For one can quickly tire of regiments of exclamation marks; one can so easily get out of breath trying to keep up with their stiff pace.

I have lingered on the subject of his voice, the pitch of his tone (the one that he would have used at Ferret-Face's table, when, holding up a spoon green with mould, he would enquire, in the most deferential manner, as if deferring to the housemaster's superior wisdom, as if genuinely anxious to know: 'Sir, have they been *digging* recently at

Uriconium?'), for they were among his strongest weapons and the most convincing vehicle, with his warm smile, of his undoubted charm. The voice had not aged, had not altered at all; it had all the freshness and natural affability of my first exposure to it, in the long, ill-lit study.

The eyes, as I have said, were also much the same, readily smiling, but perhaps more sagacious, though this may have been the effect of the learned-looking glasses. But once we had broken the ice and were talking away, as we walked from the station, it seemed to me that he had indeed grown in wisdom, a wisdom no doubt derived from experience and observation. The way he talked now of his father, the ambitious young doctor who had married for money, revealed a quality of observation that enabled him to distance himself from his own preoccupations, and fully to take in other people, especially those nearest to him, in their own right. He did not *blame* his father, he was merely stating a fact, just as when he observed that his father had wanted him to go to Uppingham rather than Shrewsbury, because he thought it would 'toughen Edward up', for he had gathered that it was a pretty sporty, rugger-playing sort of school. His only comment was that his father had lost that particular battle. I thought that many other fathers, including mine, would have expressed themselves similarly on what was good for their sons. He was now talking of his parents and his family with a certain tolerant detachment. Anyhow, I at once had the impression of a wiser, more fully-formed Edward, and one who had slowed up a good deal, was less prone to attack situations head on. Would he know about money? Would he have acquired a money sense along with a measure of worldly wisdom? His clothes were sober, but of very good quality. What had he been doing all these years? For he cannot have been travelling all the time, there must have been some sort of regular job, though I had no idea of what it might have been, save that it had always been London-based. And then there was the curious use of

French, quite good, rather staid, a bit archaic, and perhaps deliberately old-fashioned. Was this then some pale reflection of the codes that we had been in the habit of employing in the house, in order to exclude others? Not that French, however elaborate and mannered, is going to exclude anyone very much. Certainly there was a lingering element of the old theatricals in these flourished greetings and *envois*, like the carefully penned squiggles surrounding a looping signature. There was certainly nothing elaborate about his appearance: a tweed cap, sober blue mackintosh of very fine material, heavy shoes – I noticed, for the first time, how small his feet were – Harris tweed sportscoat and flannel trousers. He dressed like an OAP who would pass unnoticed among other OAPs.

Yet there remained a great deal of spontaneity, and, if now more contained, perhaps also more informed, enthusiasm, and, if we had been together longer, I suspect, the same vigorous capacity to dislike, to condemn, as to over-enthuse. He seemed still to be a person who would never do things by halves. His sense of fun, his enjoyment of provocation and outrage, had remained undimmed, and contrasted oddly with his appearance and prudent gait as an OAP. He reminded me, amidst bursts of merriment, which I soon shared, how I had rescued him from the awful heartiness of the Duke of York's Camp, an escapade of which I had had no recollection (his memory was much better than mine on the subject of our activities as schoolboys and adolescents). The whole thing had been prearranged between us, before he went off to Southwold and I, khaki-clad, to Strensall. On his second day at the camp I had sent him a telegram, presumably from York: MUM DYING COME AT ONCE DAD. With the benefit of hindsight, the message might have seemed inappropriate, even in poor taste; but it had been entirely effective at the time, which was all that mattered. It had been read to the entire assembly, at supper-time, and Edward had been taken to the station, not before one of the Duke's aides-de-camp had expressed his sympathy. I have no doubt that Edward had put on a good face till he had actually got on the train. Once in the compartment, I could imagine his convulsions of mirth. The thing had worked again. I think he then had gone to London, to stay with friends, until such time as he could decently re-emerge once the Camp had officially dispersed. I was very glad to be able to add this episode to the chronicle of our joint operations.

He also reminded me of something that I had told him once I had finally been released – I had had to stay the whole course of the ghastly tented business – from the khaki and blanco horrors of the Public Schools OTC Camp. On one of my precious visits to York, my refuge from nearby militarism, all the more comforting in its sense of pervading Quaker influence, I had gone, dressed in my untidy uniform, one or two brass buttons missing, and with no doubt my puttees trailing – I had never managed to do them up properly – to the restaurant of a big hotel to have lunch. My appearance had told so strongly against me that the head waiter had insisted that I pay for the meal in advance, before even taking my order. Edward was still very entertained by this story, which I had likewise forgotten, but which I found quite in keeping. Later, when I was in the real army, I was told by a French friend of mine, who was entertaining me in a superb Paris black market restaurant in October 1944, that I was the dirtiest soldier he had ever seen. I must have been carrying an *air de juin '40* around with me when I met my friend. I have never been able to understand why one should take pride in one's uniform, the very mark of slavery. I must say I was pleased with the York story.

I found my friend curiously understanding and, indeed, interesting about Ireland, as though, living away from the place, he had become more Irish. It was clear that, in the intervening years, he had read extensively in Anglo-Irish history. Perhaps the Irishness had always been there, just that I hadn't noticed it. It came out at once in his strongly expressed impatience with those who, during his schooldays (which, I now discovered, had begun in a preparatory school in North Wales) had suggested to him that the Irish protestants were having a bad time in the Free State, that they were being discriminated against, if not actually persecuted and physically threatened, and that they were being treated as second-class citizens. He talked of such over-simplifications, even after so many years, with obvious anger. He also described his sense of injustice when, as a boarder at Rigg's, he had been made by Ferret-Face to pay a shilling in dues on a parcel sent to him from Dublin, as a result of some anti-Irish measure taken by Customs & Excise in retaliation for the non-payment by the Free State Government of some alleged public debts. He described such pin-pricks as mean-minded, unjust, and counter-productive. We had too much to catch up on to talk about Irish history; but I had the impression that, if we had, he would have expressed his (qualified) admiration for Eamon de Valera. What was quite clear was that he had become much more interested in the past, even in history. I don't think it was just a matter of nostalgia, of looking back; I think he had given the sad history of Anglo-Irish relations a great deal of thought and that he had concluded that the faults were not all on one side. As an adolescent, he had shown a tendency to go for simple solutions and for overall judgments.

It seemed to me, too, that, while he still referred to Moloch and Medea in the old terms, and with the same half-amused familiarity, almost as if they were still little domestic demons that were liable to pop up, like grotesque creatures springing from a jack-in-the-box, in unexpected places, he had succeeded in distancing himself from the blow and counter-blow of the old family chronicle. In his tranquil assertion that his father, as a young, very ambitious, and no doubt very able doctor, had married his mother for her money, there was even more than a hint of sympathy for the latter. It sounded as if she had not had much of a time while living under his roof – and that of her sister-in-law – and that Edward was now less ready to condemn her outright. It was both a matter of distancing himself and of putting himself in the position of another, even that of his impossible mother.

I had been watching him so carefully, looking out for clues, following each lead, that it had hardly occurred to me that he might have been similarly occupied observing *me*, taking in the marks of time, registering my manner of walking, how I held myself, the way I scratched my head when nervous or when looking for a word. I had never thought of this as a game for *two*. Yet of course he could see even the back of my head. He reminded me, on this occasion, of my intense shyness as a schoolboy: when we had gone to the Villa Starkie on the coast, that time, I had been so frightened by the noise of voices raised coming from the inside, that I had refused to go in, saying that I would wait outside until he felt it was time to leave; but that he had eventually prevailed on me to go in, and that, in fact, I had much enjoyed myself and had talked my head off. Perhaps I had not given sufficient thought to the fact that our relationship, whether as schoolboys and adolescents, or over later years, could have taken the form of a *two*-way mirror.

I would have liked to have heard him talk more about his embattled and eccentric family. I felt that now he would have been capable of seeing everyone's point of view, perhaps even that of Medea. What was also evident from what he said was that he had actually *clung* to what had remained of his family, once he had returned to normal life. Perhaps *clung* is to put it too purposefully; he was too proud a man ever to have allowed himself such a gesture. It would rather have been that, having been largely deprived of family affection during childhood and adolescence, he had endeavoured to catch up on such family links as remained to him later. The death of his brother John at sixty had filled him with sadness and a sense of loss, perhaps because they had been so little together as children. Had Edward ever had much companionship from other children before going to prep school at eight? It seemed unlikely. But he had also been keen to get to know his half-sister and had since kept up with her. There had been occasions when he had met her with their father in such unpropitious venues as four-star hotels in Bournemouth or Holyhead. So he had actually *met* Moloch in later years. He spoke of his half-sister with affection and amusement, imitating her thick Dublin accent to perfection. He referred to other peoples' families as if from a lingering sense of loss and impoverishment. He spoke of my mother with a mixture of awe and affection; I had known at the time that he had not been putting on an act of overdone politeness. He had got on well with Clover's parents and sister, but a reminder of the adolescent Edward came in an amused reference to the annoyance that his mother had caused them when she had written to Clover's father as 'Canon Clover'. Trust Medea to have got it wrong, or perhaps she was buttering them up. I thought it was more likely the latter. He might now show a bit more understanding for her, but he was not going to argue that she had been in any way a tolerable person. No amount of compassion, remorse or forgiveness could ever have effected such an unlikely transformation. Indeed, he still seemed tickled at the evocation of some of Medea's extravaganzas, and gave a spirited imitation of her manner of driving the celebrated Baby Austin, taking both hands off the wheel in order to gesticulate in support of some particularly histrionic statement in the course of her effervescent conversation.

His reflective manner and his urbanity suggest that he has acquired a great deal of inner knowledge and that he has thought much about the events of his truncated life. But his letters are still curiously bald and bare, little staccato sentences and many full stops (and, of course, many exclamation marks!!!). He still writes a bit like a comic strip cartoon of the twenties and thirties, a sort of Teddy Tail style. They offer little evidence of visual appreciation, though he had spoken so eloquently of that first fortnight of freedom; perhaps, since then, he has grown tired of seeing things, and 'beyond', after so much travelling, has become like anywhere else. His letters read rather like an official bulletin for the past or coming week: Covent Garden, Sadler's Wells, this theatre or that, a couple of concerts, the Royal Festival Hall, or some minor do in St Leonards – with train-times thrown in. He is very fussy about train-times and makes the trip to St Leonards sound like a major undertaking: 'Remember, there is only *one* train an hour.' His letters show not the smallest trace of literary imagination. But then why should they? He travelled – travels – so it seems to me – like a conventional, but fussy tourist; and his accounts of his travels were as unrevealing as his brightly coloured postcards. He might have acquired a certain degree of wisdom in respect of human relations, but it did not look as if he could apply much insight to what he *saw*. A general impression is that he is rather ordinary. I used to know pretty well how to handle Edward; I am not sure whether I would now, though I am likely to find out soon enough, because he is not going to like some sections of my book. If only I could convince him that I am not attempting to judge him, but am writing out of my own recollection of things. I was, I suppose, most struck, recently, by his ordinariness. I did not feel he was the sort of person a stranger would easily remember, save perhaps as a very still, large presence at the lunch or dinner table. I am sure he would pass in a crowd, especially in an elderly one, on the front or the promenade of a seaside town. St Leonards seemed suitable, more so than Walthamstow, where he had lived previously. I wonder whether they live in a bungalow: Sea View Gardens would seem to suggest something of the kind. His neat, well-ironed clothes hinted at a tidy bungalow existence. There was about him a certain aura of fuss; and I noticed that he looked very carefully just where he put his feet, while we were walking from the station. If I went to St Leonards, I would have to wipe my shoes before going in.

Why should a convinced Wagnerian and a convicted matricide *not* be ordinary? Perhaps the fact that he is a matricide is not all that significant. Edward has grown further and further away from his crime in time, though I do not have the impression that he has made any deliberate effort to distance himself from it morally. He still talks at length about Moloch and Medea, though whether he talks about them to other people I would not know. I am a particular case, our relationship is a particular one, the two Ms are the bridge that enables him best to communicate with me in a mutually recognisable code that excludes eavesdroppers, and to refer us both back to a shared past which is apparently still very real and important to him, as, indeed, it is to me, for otherwise I would not be writing a book about it. It is perhaps significant that he should recently have taken steps to join (or re-join?) the Old Salopian Club, in an effort to catch up with the fate of his contemporaries, about some of whom he writes in each one of his letters to me. He appeared genuinely upset when I told him that Clover, Chant and Pullan had been killed in the war. Of course, he would not have known. How would he have? But now he is endeavouring to catch up. People so concerned to re-establish old links long since broken generally lead very dull lives in between. I would not be a bit surprised if he were to attend the next OS dinner to be held in London. 'And what have you been doing since we last met?' What would he say to that? Listening to Wagner? Travelling? I would not be at all surprised not just to encounter the impeccable bungalow, but garden gnomes, little windmills and tiny cannon. After all, St Helen's Road was both suburban and banal, so that what had happened there in February 1936 seems quite out of keeping with the surroundings and this somehow makes it worse. It was as if there had been a murder in a tranquil, low-keyed chronicle of everydayness, such as *The Diary of a Nobody*. But, then, if Edward had not been a murderer, would he not have been readily at home in the reassuring company of those who could be the subject of just such a diary, brought up to date to accommodate contemporary ordinariness?